Duns

**The Burgh
on the
Merse**

and surrounding villages

Duns – Burgh on the Merse

copyright ©2016 James Denham

ISBN : 978-1- 326-55908-3

With so much input from Ronald Morrison in particular and Dunse History Society in general, it gives me great pleasure to produce this book in aid of the Society.

~ Glenmore Books ~

www.glenmorebooks@yolasite.com

~ *Introduction* ~

*J*ust 45 miles south-east of Edinburgh and 15 miles to the west of Berwick, lies the old Burgh of Duns, considered one of the loveliest towns in the Borders where a fine sense of antiquity merges well within modern society. It is a town full of elegant buildings, excellent facilities and a long and interesting history. For centuries Duns and Greenlaw vied for the right to be 'capital' of Berwickshire but, since 1903, Duns was the county seat where the administrative, police and justice headquarters existed until all the changes to local government arrived. At that point, Duns lost much of its old status; but where did it all start for the old county town? Before we reach out in to that fascinating neighbourhood, it must be said, the town has been intermittently known over the centuries as Duns or Dunse or even Dunce and Douns on occasion but, while the modern name, which was also considered the original name, has been settled, the name Dunse is still used in some quarters, most particularly by the local history society. It must also be mentioned, every document relating to the town's origins and possibly some knowledge of pre-historic times, was lost in the burnings of the town during the 16th century.

*D*uns does, however, have an invigorating, timeless aura about it and that feeling is everywhere around the town centre. While it is a modern society, it still retains the appearance and dignity of an earlier age. It does have an air of importance but it is by no means aloof nor dismissal of the many, welcome visitors.

*T*he situation of the town, near the English Border, meant attacks were always, 'just over the horizon' and so often, the people had to regroup and build their town anew. The town we now see, retains a layout which was created from the late 16th century onwards. It is the layout of an old Scottish Burgh, a layout which, over the centuries, has served its purpose well and indeed, still does. So no matter from what direction we enter the enter the town, we inevitably arrive at the Market Square.

*W*here appropriate, some notes on the wider history of Scotland have been mentioned particularly where they affected Duns and Berwickshire. I have also used, inevitably, several tracts from my previous books on the Ridings' Festivals and Village Kirks of the Borders in order to 'keep the flow' You will also find articles from the Dunse History Society.

*W*e also take a look at surrounding villages and a couple of interesting 'farm towns' as we make our way along the Merse and north towards the Lammermuirs. Finally, thanks to Ronald Morrison and the Dunse History Society for all the practical support. I do hope you find this offering as interesting as I did during research.

*F*inally I would like to apologise for the quality of some of the photographs. Many old and some new, do not take kindly to normal paper but it is still important, in my humble opinion, to include them nonetheless.

My best regards, James.

~ Acknowledgements ~

*Taff Hurlow *Bill Law
*David Morrison *William Dobie
*Charlotte Dobie *Carol Trotter
*Doug Smith *Ian Paterson
*Heather Waldron *Ronald Morrison
*Rod Thomson *Ray Davidson *Lee Davies
*Maggie Maan *Marjorie Home
*Pauline Burbidge *Charlie Poulson
*Heather Gibson *Cat Macdonald-Home
*David Home *Walter Baxter
*Agnes Anderson   *Mike Hardy
*John Rogerson *Graham Robson
*David Spry *Becky Williamson
*Brian Turner *Jim Barton *Ben Brooksbank
*Lisa Jarvis *James T M Towill. *James Allan
*James Allan *Brian Turner *John Church
and to my wife, Elizabeth, for her patience and encouragement.

Thank you to you all for the help you have given. If I have omitted anyone, it is an error on my part and am truly sorry.

Photographs

Photographs from Geograph
While most have been given by the author, it is still important to add the relevant license.

So many of the photographs in this book, including my own and Walter Baxter's have appeared on the Geograph Project. They have been published here under the Creative Commons Attribution ShareAlike 2.0 Generic License. Furthermore, all photographs shown without credit are copyright of the author.

Photographs from the Wikpedia Project are repruduced under the Creative Commons Attribution ShareAlike 3.0 Unreported 2.5 Generic 2.0 Generic 1.0 Generic License (Wikipedia Commons)

~ Contents ~

9..........................Duns – In the beginning
11..Christianity to Burgh
20..........................Century of Doom
27...A New Beginning
45..........................Today's Town
57..Annual Events
66..........................Notable People
68..Today's Churches
76..........................Great Houses
99..Abbey St. Bathans
103..........................Allanton, Allanbank, Broomdykes
112..Bonkyl, Preston, Lintlaw
120..........................Chirnside, Chirnsidebridge
132..Cranshaws
137..........................Edrom, Blanerne
142..Fogo
148..........................Gavinton
153..Greenlaw
164..........................Longformacus, Whitchester, Ellemford
178..Polwarth
182..........................Swinton, Simprim
190..Whitsome, Hilton

Duns from the Law
©Brian Turner - Geograph

~ *Duns – Burgh on the Merse* ~

~ *In the Beginning* ~

*T*here are no reliable dates available to indicate when man first set foot in Scotland and some estimates vary wildly with variations of tens of thousands of years though recently in Norfolk, finds were made, estimating man first walked on the lands which were to become known as Britain, some 950,000 years ago. When man first made the trip north to Scotland is not known.

*T*here is very little knowledge of language nor writings from pre-historic times and experts must rely on what is found, in the form of archaeology, burials, weapons and everyday utensils. Some of the best results for Berwickshire or, more importantly Duns, arrived in 2013 when the water board were carrying out improvements to the water supply near Duns Law when, during their excavations, they discovered the cremated body of a woman with more human bones, a quantity of beakers and a stone axe. Experts later estimated the find was some 4,500 years old fitting in almost perfectly with the time the Gudoddin tribe are thought to have arrived in what became south-east Scotland, circa 3,500 - 2,500BC. Perhaps the most important part of the water board find was the fact, it was found just outwith the protected area of historical note! It must be said however, the Gododdin were not necessarily the first 'visitors' to the area, it is thought other nomadic tribes of hunter-gatherers passed through even earlier on their never ending search for food...and safety.

*T*he Gododdin people (later known to the Romans as the Votadini) were known to build their homes within a hilltop fort or Dun (Dyn) as protection against would-be insurgents. Preferably the hill would have thick tree cover for further protection and a ready supply of wood for their fires and there is very little doubt those were the first people to actually settle in that part of the country. Their views to the south, from the Law, where the dangers lay, would be extensive, viewing as they did, the great plain of the Merche, or Merse.

A CAIRN ON THE LAW
This stone cairn with bench seat, situated on the southern edge of the hill fort is sign posted on the approach path as the orientation point. A plaque provides information on the history around Duns Law
© Walter Baxter

~ *In the Beginning* ~

Life for the settlement would be as ideal as it could possibly be in those early times when food and refreshment was plentiful in the surrounding woods and nearby waters and, for the most part, that situation would remain unchanged for hundreds of years. Bears, wolves and badgers were plentiful so materials for clothing were 'at hand' while wild cattle, sheep and hogs wandered freely and would provide more for clothing and food. The people of the 'dun' above the Merse were subordinate to their king, who resided at Dun or Dyn Pelydr (Traprain Law) to the north and they would certainly follow in the traditional habits and ritual of their own kith and kin, worshipping their Gods including perhaps, Baal, the great God of Fire, in their own time honoured fashion They also had, what for us would be a more than strange custom which was enacted out at the Winter Equinox and Summer Solstice, when the young people danced around the hill, entirely naked, as a means of enhancing their fertility; they also believed in fairies who were said to steal their clothes during their ritual.

In the later years of the 1st century AD, the Roman Legions arrived and, though they built their principal route, Dere Street, from York to Inveresk, a route to the west of Duns, they did build a road cutting off Dere Street at Rochester, heading for Berwick and that did bring them closer to Duns meaning there is no reason not to believe, they 'visited' the Votadini people of the Law. In fact the Romans are said to have struck a 'deal' with the tribe's elders at Traprain, therefore it is reasonable to believe there was no bloodshed at Duns. Other hillforts using the name 'dun' in the south-east included, Din (Dyn) Eidyn (Edinburgh) Dyn Bar, Dun Law and Eildon, or, in old, 'Heel dun or doun' joining countless other hillforts and enclosures with the prefix 'Dun'

As the years passed, the old fort was becoming too small and unfit for purpose meaning more homes had to be built around a great morass at the foot of the hill, slightly to the west, and that new settlement too was protected by another, perhaps smaller fort, a fort which may have some significance as we shall learn in later paragraphs. While the settlement grew, the future held no guarantees for the people's safety. In time, the Roman Legions departed the scene and, for up to two centuries, the people lived in relative peace apart from sporadic fighting when fending off Pictish raids from the north and the constant annoyances from the Selgovae to the west. As if they didn't have their sorrows to seek, more dangerous breeds were beginning to conquest the north-east of England and south-east Scotland, an area which soon became known as *Hen Ogledd (Old North)*

~ *Arrival of Christianity to Burgh of Barony* ~

Before the 6th century was out, the remnants of the Brythonic people of the Goddodin or Goutodin, had been overrun by the Angles and Saxons from the south forming their own kingdom of Bernicia which consisted of most of the Gudoddin lands including modern day Northumberland, County Durham, Berwickshire and East Lothian. The so called Dark Ages had come and gone and the early Middle Ages were upon us and life was about to get very difficult for the people of the Law. It is important to mention, the people of the town, did <u>not</u> run away when the invaders arrived, they simply, in time, 'blended' in with many of the new arrivals and cross tribe marriages would surely take place. Barely two centuries later, Bernicia united with its southern neighbour Deira to form the new Kingdom of Northumbria. The first monarch of that new kingdom was Oswald, a man who actively promoted Christianity and, during his reign, he contributed greatly to the new commune at Lindisfarne until his death in 642AD. From Lindisfarne, men like Aiden, Baldred, Boisel the Confessor and Cuthbert brought the new faith to what we now know as Scotland. As well as those four *Holy Pilgrims of the Holy Island,* the king, Oswald, was canonised within the Catholic Church.

Christianity had arrived but more trouble was on the horizon. From before 872AD, the Kingdom of Northumbria including, of course, Dunse, was under the iron fist rule of the Vikings. Those foreign seafarers knew only one way of life, to pillage, plunder and kill, meaning for the next century, the people of Dunse lived in constant fear. In 941 AD, the Vikings thrust through much of Berwickshire ravaging every toun and ecclesiastical compound they could find on their way. That barbaric raid finally ended at Auldhame in modern day East Lothian when their king, Olaf Guthfrithsson, who reigned as King of Dublin and York from 934 – 941AD, was killed and buried in the kirkyard in St. Baldred's Church at that village, just south of North Berwick. Digs were made in 2014 and the team of archaeologists had little doubt of the king's identity when they found his grave. No sooner had the Norsemen retreated to Dublin the iron fisted Angle rulers of Northumbria stepped back in to the 'driving seat'

As we know, in those far off, stormy days, Scotland was far from the country we now know. The south-east was in Northumbria, south-west in the ancient Kingdom of Strathclyde, the north was divided between Pictland (or as the Romans named it, Caledonia) and Dalriada, home of the Scots. The united northern nations of Picts and Scots finally overpowered Strathclyde but it would take until the Battle of Carham in 1018 to bring Berwickshire, officially, in to the Kingdom of Scotland. Even then it was barely recognised as being Scottish though some Scottish kings did take some interest but not so much in the case of David I who reigned from 1124 until 1153.

Many believed David was a pious man and perhaps he was, but he was also known to be a power hungry man. Some thought he built castles and endowed monasteries and abbeys as a show of power and sophistication to the English

~ *Christianity to Burgh* ~

but David had no need to impress his English cousins. He grew up at the court of his uncle, Henry I, held two earldoms in England and more lands in Normandy. He brought hundreds of Norman allies with him from their bases in Normandy which was then part of England, to help impose his will on Scotland. His mission was a show of power and strength to the Scottish people and his adversaries in the north of the country; he was known to look upon the people of East Lothian and Berwickshire as still not Scottish and he often referred to them as English. If we look at all the great churches David founded across the land, he paid little attention to East Lothian or Berwickshire. So many of the churches of the south-east, owe their existence to those devout holy men of Lindisfarne who trudged the coastline, the Merse and across the Lammermuirs, spreading the Gospel and the Good Word to the people of Berwickshire and Haddingtonshire.

Whether David acknowledged Dunse and Berwickshire or not, he did bring a new form of order to his kingdom which affected everyone in Scotland for ever more. He introduced a new pecking order, a legal system, a parochial system leading to parish division and ultimately, counties. He introduced a laird or lord to every manor who generally took the name of his manor and, in the case of Dunse, the lairds were known simply as 'de Dunse' (or, of Duns)

The 12th June, 1152, during David's reign, is one of the earliest known mentions of Duns, now a thriving village, when Hugo de Duns, perhaps the vicar and almost certainly of Grueldykes, witnessed a charter given by Roger d'Eu or d'Ow, of Langton, when that lord granted the church at Langton with all its facilities and perpetual alms, to Kelso Abbey, for the salvation of the soul of Earl Henry, (son of King David) his ancestors and descendants. Hugo, almost certainly of Norman descent, went on to witness more charters in slightly later times but more is known of John of Duns who witnessed so many charters in the 1190s. Mention too, is made of another Hugo, who was described as a forester in a charter of North Durham. (Coldingham) while Patrick of Duns, said to be the first known chaplain at Duns, appears in documents of 1165 and is later mentioned in three charters of Coldingham. Robert of Duns was a chaplain at Birnie in Moray, and was thought to have been transferred there after the death of the bishop but before the arrival of the new dean of Moray, Freskin, in 1203; it may be the case, Robert was a chaplain at Duns before his transfer north. In the 1280s, Henry of Lemmington, sometimes designated Henri de Lemmaton, was another chaplain at Duns Church before becoming a parson in Doune, Perthshire, a town he represented at Berwick in 1296 when he performed the act fealty to Edward I of England before later being appointed Chancellor to the King, Robert Bruce. Henri was an interesting character in as much that, he refused to swear fealty to Edward in 1292 and was thought to have been 'released' from his post at Dunse, then here we see him actually paying fealty on behalf of another parish

~ *Christianity to Burgh* ~

in 1296. That 'notable honour' of performing the act of fealty in 1296 on behalf of Duns, was carried out by Robert de Duns, again possibly a member of the local noble family or, more likely, the clergy (or perhaps both) The next chaplain at the church was another Henry, this one designated thus, 'de Monckton'.

James Robson speculated a church was in place before the end of David I's reign in 1153 which may indicate the aforementioned Hugo was, in actual fact, the parson of the kirk. Another mention of the church arrived before the end of the 12th century when it was listed in the Ancient Taxatio with a value of 110 merks underlining the church's early importance. It was further included in the Bagimund's Rolls of 1274. Other men of whom we know from the pre-Reformation Church are, Adam who was Rector in 1374, Michael Ker who was the vicar in 1490 and Sir John Clark who was vicar-pensioner in 1529 when he was ably assisted by his curate, Patrick Morrison.

In those early years, from the mid 13th century, the church was thought to have been under the jurisdiction of the *Bona Hospitalis de Duns* situated close to Duns Mill though that cannot be wholly substantiated though another chapel and hospital in the parish situated to the north, on lands now known as Chapel Farm, was dedicated to St. Mary Magdalene which makes sense since many hospital chapels all over Europe were so dedicated in that saint's name. Numerous mentions of that establishment appear over the years, even beyond the Reformation. In 1611, attempts were made to create a separate parish at Birkenside as the Chapel area was then known, with the 'Kirklands of Ellem' being granted to the chapel as a 'sweetener' but the proposal fell through. From that point Birkenside Chapel fell in to ruin and, in time, both church and graveyard were cleared during farming operations. We know of two men in association with Birkenside, Thomas Young who was Parson Principal in 1394 and Edward Cockburn who's castle lay nearby, was Master of the Hospital in 1492.

In the midst of all that, was a birth, in 1266, of, perhaps the town's greatest son, John of Duns, better known as John Duns Scotus who was a member of the local lordly family of Grueldykes. His uncle, Elias de Dunse, fought for the autonomy of the Franciscan movement in Scotland and later became Vicar-General of the Scottish Franciscans. Only wealthy men were able to be educated in, and be part of a religious order in those early days which gives further indication of the powerful family in the area. John of Dunse later followed in his uncle's footsteps, first being educated by Elias himself, before entering the Franciscan school at Haddington then on to Oxford and Paris. In time, 'Scotus' was added to his name as a further form of recognition of his roots as he travelled the length and breadth of Europe.

John Duns Scotus became a priest, and, in time, one of the most influential churchmen and philosophers of his time. Though he never joined a Franciscan

~ *Christianity to Burgh* ~

Priory in the normal sense, preferring to work in the wider community and the major seats of learning, he was still very much a Franciscan and is much revered by that brotherhood. Because of his far reaching views and forward thinking, many thought John a trifle foolish and, in time, his name, Dunse, became synonymous with silly or foolish students thus the word 'dunce or dunse' being introduced to the English language. John was beatified by Pope John Paul II in 1993, entitling him the Blessed John Duns Scotus.

*H*e influenced so much of the Catholic Church's thinking and many believe, so many of his views would still be considered 'before his time' in the present day. John died in Cologne on 8th November, 1308 and is interred in the Franscican Church of Minorities of the Immaculate Conception near Cologne Cathedral. His life is fondly remembered by the Franciscans who have built two monuments to him in the place of his birth, one in the public park and another at the Pavilion entrance to the castle on the spot where many believe he was born; more recognition of the great man can be seen at the Church of Our Lady Immaculate and St. Margaret in the town. John of Duns must surely be considered one of the truly great Scots, a man of intellectual genius and, though he was probably born centuries too early, his work and genius will live forever. 2016 marks the 750th anniversary of the great man's birth and there is no doubt, many celebrations will be held in his honour across the whole of Christendom including of course, where his roots lay at the place of his birth, Dunse. In time, we shall discuss Duns Castle but it is probable, there would be some form of lordly house, probably fortified, before the present castle and its known forerunners were built. As we have seen, the town was growing, the church had been founded and where there was a church, a town and a laird, there would surely be some form of lordly house, especially since, in those early times, Duns lay on a very important route...a route often used by the unwanted, the *Border Reivers,* on both sides of the border. Among the most famous, or notorious if you like, of all the Berwickshire reivers, were the Home family and the Trotters of Prentannan, many a 'fine' tale has emanated from their activities. It is said however, most of their reiving was done on the other side of the border but there is no doubt some skullduggerry was still carried out on home soil.

~ *Christianity to Burgh* ~

Across:

John Duns Scots Memorial in Public Park

Right:

John Duns Scotus' Tomb in the Church of Minorities in Cologne courtesy of Ronald Morrison

Another castle to the west, Borthwick Castle, was thought to have been built in a higher position as a lookout for the laird's house to the south-east. That castle, probably more of an L shaped watchtower with a surrounding barmkin, was the property of the powerful Cockburns of Langton. Sadly the castle was not yet in place when men of evil arrived in 1292 and 1296, following on from Edward the Hammer's visits to Berwick when, on both occasions, he demanded the allegiance of the powerful men and clergy of Scotland. That dastardly king must have had the thought, "Since I am in Scotland, I may as well cause some damage" and he did! with Berwickshire, including Dunse, taking the brunt of his wrath on both occasions. In spite of his anger, Dunse continued to grow in both size and importance and, in time, Scottish royalty would take notice.

A year after the Battle of Bannockburn, King Robert camped his army at Duns probably more as a warning to the English since no assault on England was made. Soon after, the king granted lands at Dunse to one of his trusted lieutenants, Thomas Randolph, 1st Earl of Moray, said to be the king's nephew and, by 1318, he was making his mark, assembling an army at Duns, with the help of Sir James Douglas (the good Sir James) and Patrick, Earl of Dunbar and March, before attacking and re-taking Berwick from the English. In 1320, Randolph began work on building the first, known, stone tower at Duns which would prove to be the first of several works and rebuilds leading to the magnificent, castellated mansion-house we see today. However, there is a strong belief, Randolph's castle was by no means the first. We noted earlier the extension to the fort on the law. As numbers outgrew the fort on the hill, another fort was built to the west; Duns Castle is to the west and there is every reason to believe, the Votadini or their immediate descendants, may have built the first fortification on or near the site of the present castle.

~ *Christianity to Burgh* ~

*I*n 1328, the new laird built the town's first tolbooth where miscreants could be tried and securely held if appropriate. The laird's chancellor, or provost, was appointed to oversee the tolbooth and soon, the general organisation of the town became what appears to be akin to the beginnings of local government. In 1329, Randolph became Regent of Scotland on the death of the king who died at Cardross, a king, it is believed, who had visited his trusty servant at Duns on several occasions.

*T*homas Randolph was second only to the king, in the queue to sign the Declaration of Arbroath in 1320 before, in 1322, travelling to Rome to attend the Papal court where he won temporary absolution for the king who had previously been excommunicated for the murder of the Comyn at Dumfries. Moray died at Musselburgh in 1332 when leading an army to repel an attack on Berwickshire by Edward Baliol. Interestingly Thomas Randolph was married to Isabel Stewart, sister of Sir John Stewart of Bonkyl who died at the Battle of Falkirk in 1298 in support of William Wallace. Coincidentally, only a year earlier, after several clashes in Northumbria, sorties which ended at Berwick, Wallace's army passed through Duns on their way home before their leader was declared Guardian of Scotland at, thought by some, Selkirk Old Kirk.

*I*n July 1333, only a year after the death of Moray, Edward de Baliol, son of the disgraced King John, occupied Berwick with much help from Edward III of England, grandson of the 'Hammer'. Now that King Robert Bruce and his lieutenant-in-chief, Randolph of Moray, had died, the window of opportunity opened for the de Baliols and, with the help of the English, attempted to regain some of their tattered dignity, redress the balance after Bannockburn...and take the throne of Scotland.

*A*rchibald Douglas had assembled a great army of Scots which marched south overnight to face the rebels' and English threat. The Scots' army rested at Duns Law before the march to Berwick the next day. In the morning, the 19th July, 1333, they set out for Berwick, but nearing Halidon Hill, Douglas quickly realised, de Baliol's forces had already taken the high ground and attack would be suicidal but attack he did. The Scots were torn apart and soon in utter disarray causing them to flee the scene, only the Ross Highlanders stood their ground before falling to a man. Douglas, the young King's Regent, along with many more of the Scots' nobility, was killed as were countless hundreds of his men. Halidon Hill, was not quite on the same scale as Flodden some two centuries later, but the battered, bedraggled foot soldiers who survived, would be thanking God on their way back towards Duns, but distraught by the fact, south-east Scotland was, once again, firmly in the greedy grip of the English, ably assisted by 'Scottish' rebels.

*D*uring that campaign, Edward III granted the castle and lands at Dunse to Sir Thomas de Bradeston, his most trusted general but it is unlikely de

~ *Christianity to Burgh* ~

Bradeston lived at the castle for any period of time. He was an interesting character and, as the Governor of Berkeley Castle, was said to be complicit in the murder of Edward II at Berkeley in 1327.

Bradeston, of Whiston in Gloucester, was later created 1st Lord Bradeston but it is not known if he was involved in his king's fifth invasion of Scotland in 1356 when the intention was to burn every church they came across which almost certainly included Duns Church, during an invasion which became known at the *Burnt Candlemas.*

In April, 1342, Dunbar Church of St. Bae (Bega) was created a Collegiate Church by George, Earl of Dunbar and March, with the blessing of the king, David II and the pope, Benedict XII. Within weeks of that church's new status, Dunse Church was created one of its prebends, a title which was held until soon after the Reformation in 1560.

Plaque at the site of the
Battle of Halidon Hill
Courtesy of Lisa Jarvis©2007

Dunbar Collegiate had eight prebendary churches, including Duns and Chirnside, and employed eight canons, one assigned to each prebend. Each canon, in order to receive funds and reimbursement, was expected to live in the vicinity of his charge.

One man who is known to have visited Duns Church on many occasions during his reign of the 14th century, was Columba de Dunbar, the Dean of the College.

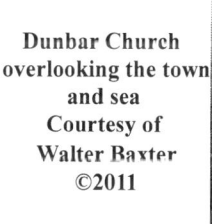

Dunbar Church overlooking the town and sea
Courtesy of Walter Baxter
©2011

~ *Christianity to Burgh* ~

While there was a period when the Earls of Dunbar and March lost control of their lands to the Crown, the church at Dunbar still retained many powers over the church at Duns.

In those early days and indeed from the 12th century, and for some time beyond, while not the lairds of the manor as such, the Earls of Dunbar, sometimes styled March or Lothian and ancestors of the Home family, wielded much power in the region as a whole.

They came to Scotland in the late 11th century and were granted extensive lands by King Malcolm III and his son Edgar, bearing in mind, Berwickshire still had more in common with Northumbria than the rest of Scotland; it is no coincidence, the first 'of Dunbar' was Cospatric who was the Earl of Northumbria up to that point. Their involvement in Dunbar and the Marches of Berwickshire would affect every sphere of everyday life of the citizens and their church and still their blood flows across the lands in and around the great Merse.

The most notable, and enduring, of all events at Old Dunse is the *'Legend of the Dingers'* In 1377, Henry Percy, 1st Earl of Northumberland, headed north, hell bent on causing yet more damage on the hard pressed people of Berwickshire. One night during his foraging, he set up camp at Duns Wood leaving, of course, sentries around his sleeping soldiers. Some local lads crept upon the slumbering host but were more interested in the horses paddocked a short distance away. The locals brought with them their cattle rattles which were made of dried animal skin, held together with thin pieces of wood and filled with pebbles. They were intent on chasing the horses which they did by 'dinging' their rattles, creating a great noise amidst the still of the night. The frightened horses panicked and galloped off awakening the soldiers in the process. The soldiers, confused and frightened in the total darkness, took to flight, some it is said, being killed on their way over what became known as the Bloody or Bluidy Burn. Whether they were killed or not is of no consequence, the locals returned to the town with the cry *"Duns dings a"* (Duns beats all) - a legend was born and the nickname of the townsfolk was created, 'Dingers' as the locals are still known, is carried with pride by everyone born in the town, and their cry embraces the town's Coat of Arms.

Probably the greatest moment in the town's history however, arrived towards the end of the 15th century when, at the behest of the young king, James IV, Duns was elevated to Burgh of Barony in 1489 with the official presentation of the Charter to the lairds, George Home of Ayton and his son John. This meant the town was now able to hold fairs including a week long fair between Pentecost and Trinity Sunday, and weekly markets enabling the tradesmen and farmers of the time to increase business and attract new investment. Now the Barons possessed the right to appoint a Baron-Baillie and Burgesses and, in time, Bailiffs. A Mercat Cross was erected, to mark the

~ *Christianity to Burgh* ~

town's proud new status and great opportunities arrived which were grabbed with willing hands, commerce improved, agriculture improved and markets thrived, but sadly, it would all end in disaster for the old town during the course of the next 80 years. The new market cross however, would not only be the focal point of simply fairs, markets or merriment, it would one day be the scene of one the most macabre events, as we shall see.

As a matter of note, just a few years, in 1496, after he raised Duns to Burgh of Barony status, the king, James IV. visited the town with his nobles to meet the assembled lords of the south to convene a meeting. A form of Parliament was enacted in an area which later became known as Parliament Close, on a site which became known as Castle Wynd, now the southern section of Castle Street; it's said, a planned attack on England was abandoned at that meeting.

**South section of Castle Street
near the site of Parliament Square and the King's Entry**

In 1497 however, the Scots, without their king, invaded Northumbria but were quickly repelled by local forces which were later reinforced by another 'Hammer of the Scots' Thomas Howard, 1st Earl of Surrey. He dispersed the Scottish army before chasing them in to Berwickshire. Many towns, including Duns and Chirnside were plundered before he captured Ayton Castle.

The end of the 15th century had arrived, the church was growing, Christianity was well established across the nation, and the town, now a Burgh of Barony, market town and Berwickshire's most important town, was well and truly established; the only element missing within the thriving community, was peace and that was still a dream, consigned to the distant future.

~ *A Century of Doom* ~

Without doubt, the 16th century was the darkest period in Scotland's history, so many Scots died, towns torched and churches and abbeys laid bare. Dunse suffered as much, if not more than many but through the eerie mists of burning embers, a ray of hope finally appeared on the horizon as we shall learn in future paragraphs.

It all began at Flodden in 1513 when the king, James IV, and thousands of his young men died on the killing fields near Branxton; every town and village, particularly in southern Scotland, suffered as a nation's young men perished, but those *Flo'ers o' the Forest* stood tall, shoulder to shoulder with their king as they crossed the river and entered Paradise as one. September 9th 1513 is the blackest date in Scottish history, a date many wished to see erased from the calendar...forever.

That battle ended what had been a successful campaign for the king and his army. It didn't seem so long since the troops were mustered at Ellemford just to the north, where many men of the old town enlisted in the Royal Army.

The haugh lands on both sides of the ford were awash with Scots soldiers as the king and his bishops attended the church on the left bank of the river. King James then addressed his army before they set off on their invasion of North England, many never to return

Ellemford Bridge

After taking and destroying the castles at Ford, Etal and Norham, the king was confident of more success. News filtered through of a great army, led by the Earl of Surrey, marching on Branxton and James decided to meet them head on. On the day, the Scots held the high ground but for some unknown reason, perhaps over confidence, they descended the hill to face the English head on...the outcome was a disaster.

In terms of numbers, that was the biggest battle ever enacted between the historic foes and, again in terms of numbers, it was Scotland's heaviest ever defeat. No one really knows how many died, but it was thought, there were 1,500 English casualties while around 10,000 Scots met their maker. Those were dark times indeed but there was even more low points still to come.

~ *A Century of Doom* ~

The Church of St. Paul at Branxton

Many priests tended the wounded and dying Scots in the wake of the Battle of Branxton Moor, or, as the Scots know it, Flodden Field. So many of the dead were laid to rest in a neighbouring burial site

The true extent of the numbers of dead will never be known but what is known is, so many Scots' Lords of the realm died with King James including John Hay, 2nd Lord Yester and George, 5th Lord Seton both ancestors of the Hay family of Duns Castle. Indeed the Hays, it is said, can claim to be of royal blood, with descent from Robert III, by way of John Hay, 1st of Yester who's maternal grandmother was Princess Mary, daughter of Robert III of Scots.

One aristocrat who did not die was Alexander, 3rd Lord Home, Chamberlain to the King and Warden of the Eastern March. Less than four weeks before Flodden, Home led his cavalry in to Northumbria and did a lot of damage and 'collected' much booty as he rampaged his way through village after village. The Earl of Surrey contacted his northern commander, Sir William Bulmer, Warden of the East March in Northumberland, to search for the intruders. Bulmer and his much smaller force caught up with the Berwickshire men at Millfield near Wooller, resulting in the almost inevitable English victory with, it is said, Home losing 1,000 men at the battle. however he did manage to re-assemble forces in time to march with the king to Flodden. On the day, Home's cavalry cut through the English right flank but when he ordered his battalion to change course and assist the rest of the king's army, he left the scene. In time, Home did not accept Albany, the new Regent for the infant, James V, and was made forfeit of his posts, finally being executed with his brother, William, by beheading, with their heads pinned to spikes at the Tolbooth in Edinburgh.

The king's son, James V, was barely a year old when his father perished and a regent, the aforementioned Duke of Albany, (John Stewart) uncle of the late king, was appointed to govern the country during the young king's infancy but that in its own led to problems, one of which arrived on Dunse's doorstep.

~ A Century of Doom ~

During Albany's reign, the most ignoble incident in Duns' history, arrived in 1517 and the tale of the demise of de la Bastie, the new Warden of the Eastern Marches. Albany, who had grown up in France, brought many of his friends from that country to fill high office in the government of Scotland...one of those friends was Antoine d'Arces or d'Argie, le seigneur de la Bastie. De la Bastie cut a dashing figure, a veteran of continental wars, he was universally acclaimed as the man to put an end to constant feuding around the Merse and the so called lawlessness of the Home and Trotter families and others.

Let us have a look at the following excerpt from an article provided by the Dunse History Society.

Murder of Chevalier de la Bastie
Broomhouse near Duns. 20th September, 1517.

.......By and large, "Albany proved not an unsuccessful Governor but tensions were growing. There were those who felt war should be pursued vigorously invoking French assistance while others, mindful of Flodden, which was now being recognised more and more for the disaster it was, felt more inclined to abandon the French alliance and pursue a policy of co-operation with the English. Also, Albany's French followers were proving unpopular and the running costs of the Court unacceptably high.

There were a number of Lords opposed to Albany's rule but by and large he managed to win them over with the exception of the Earl of Hume, the strongest magnate in the south-east of Scotland who was later executed (with his brother) and deprived of his office of Warden of the East March. The Humes' loyalty had been questioned before. They had been instrumental in the uprising against James III resulting in his death at Sauchieburn and some accounts question the full extent of their commitment at Flodden. In 1517, Albany returned to France leaving in charge, to preside over a council of regency of four earls, his deputy, Chevalier de la Bastie, a handsome devil by all accounts hence his nickname, Beauté

The Bastie Memorial Monument
Courtesy of Walter Baxter

22

~ *A Century of Doom – de la Bastie* ~

*T*he Hume family naturally resented the execution of the earl and the loss of their wardenship.

*I*n a dispute over the inheritance to the Estate of Langton, William Cockburn, who was married to a Hume, who claimed the title and is described as a 'brisk man' was, with his brother-in-law, Hume of Wedderburn, laying siege to Langton Castle. De la Bastie, who was in Kelso, summoned Wedderburn to meet with him and they met two miles north of Kelso and journeyed together, at first, it seemed amicably, until they had reached a spot somewhere around present day Gavinton where a violent disagreement broke out. La Bastie felt obliged to flee for his life seeking to return to his castle at Dunbar. He fled through the streets of Duns pursued by Wedderburn and other kinsmen who had left from besieging Langton and joined in the chase. As de la Bastie crossed the Whiteadder at Broomhouse, his horse fell and although defending valiantly, he was overcome and slain by John Home of Manderston and Patrick Hume, brother of David Hume of Wedderburn.

*L*a Bastie's head was cut off and exposed on Dunse Market Cross. His body was buried where he fell and a cairn was later erected by Patrick Hume of Broomhouse.

*I*n due course, the head was removed from the cross but remained at Wedderburn Castle until 1810 when it was burned by Miss Jean Hume.

*O*n 19th February the following year, sentence of forfeiture was brought against the Humes and shortly afterwards a force under the Earl of Arran marched against them. No battle ensued however, the Humes effectively surrendering at Lauder and handing over the keys to the castles of Hume, Langton and Wedderburn on the promise of a pardon.

*I*n 1975, the present monument to Antoine d'Arcy de la Bastie was erected by Berwickshire Civic Society……………………………….

*N*igel Tranter, in his book, *The Border Country,* described the Home or Hume family as akin to the *Grand Army of Mexico,* where there always appeared to be more generals than privates. Little is heard of the lesser known members of the family but the ones we do know of, were indeed a powerful family and, of course, they were not always right in whatever they were involved in but that does not mean to say they were always wrong and many did, over the years, fight unselfishly for their country and the common weal of the people. They did provide for the people of the Merse and wherever else they controlled and indeed, much of what we see today is or was of their making, indeed, Baron Home of Ayton, who received the Barony of Duns in 1489, did so much for the furtherance of the small community which grew to be Berwickshire's principal town.

*T*oday, there is a Clan Home Society with the current chief, David Alexander Cospatrick Douglas-Home, 15th Earl of Home. He is descended

~ *A Century of Doom* ~

from the original Cospatric, Earl of Northumbria who himself, is said to be descended from the Royal House of both England and Scotland, from William I (the Conquerer) or Alfred the Great, and Macbeth. The present chief is the son of the former Prime Minister of the United Kingdom, Sir Alex. Douglas-Home. The name Cospatric was synonymous with most of the early progress of Berwickshire and, through his descendants, the Home family and many others of note.

*A*fter the de la Bastie affair was long gone, things began to settle down again but only briefly, allowing the citizens of Dunse to get on with their lives, and the new burgh thrived as never before; business around the market place boomed and that in itself was attracting more and more people to the town below the hill which was beginning to reach down towards the church. It seemed everything was going to plan, a growing market town, growing prosperity and growing confidence but that was about to change...yet again!

*O*n 8th December, 1542, at Linlithgow Palace, James V's wife, Marie (de Guise) gave birth to a daughter whom the royal couple named Mary or, Marie, in tribute to her mother. Little did the couple know, that birth would not only change the face of Scottish history but the entire history of the island of Britain, perhaps one of most fateful turning points in world history. All the important eyes in Christendom were on Scotland and none more so than the King of England, Henry Tudor, eighth of the name and a man desperate to rule the world. He changed all the rules of law, of marriage, of church and engagement in his own country and was determined to extend his kingdom both to the south and the north. There was no limit to his ambition and he would stop at nothing to achieve his goal.

Linlithgow Palace with St. Michael's Kirk beyond, where Queen Mary was born and baptised copyright of Viktor Paulk - Wikpedia Project

*W*hen Princess Mary was born, he seized on an idea to marry his own son, Edward, just five years old, to the baby girl who's father died only six days after her birth, in the wake of the Battle of Solway Moss

*O*ver the next few years, Henry made overtures to the Royal Family of

~ *A Century of Doom* ~

Scotland and to the Scottish Estates (Parliament) to that end but his patience eventually ran out. In 1544, it became a heavily pressing matter and the real 'wooing' of the Scottish Court began in earnest with Berwickshire being the first region to suffer. Henry did not take the Regent of Scotland, Marie de Guise, too seriously, but she was an able sovereign in her own right and would bow to no one, least of all Henry of England. She had a determination to see the good fight through to the bitter end, and as we are about to see, she triumphed over the evil English monarch who died, taking his dreams and ambitions with him to his grave in St. George's Chapel at Windsor Castle.

In the early months of 1544, Edward Seymour, brother-in-law of King Henry, led a huge force, spread across southern Scotland, burning and looting wherever they went. Sir George Bowes led a filter group towards the small town of Duns which suffered badly when the English freebooters struck, causing so much damage and carnage, not to mention death of the local people. Again, in 1545, the townspeople suffered the same heartbreaking fate, as did Duns Castle, just as they were beginning to recover from their trauma of a year earlier. At that point, many attempted to rebuild while others moved home to various villages in the area. Others began to build further south on the site of the present town but in the main, most attempted to restore what they had lost. Sadly the attacks were not over and yet more were to come in 1547 leading to the Battle of Pinkie before the English retreat from Haddington across the Lammermuirs with their tails between their legs, yet they still found time to cause even more heartache at Duns.

THIS STONE MARKS THE SITE OF THE OLD TOWN OF DUNSE DESTROYED IN THE BORDER RAIDS OF 1588

Courtesy of Walter Baxter

The last major attack of 1558, duly arrived, causing so much more damage which proved the end of the old town which was later referred to as the 'burnt town' or *Bruntons* as it is now known. If there was any consolation for the Scottish people, their beloved Princess Mary did not marry Edward, her mother saw to that and the Scots had survived. The earlier Treaty of Haddington between Scotland and France was signed and Mary went on to

~ *A Century of Doom* ~

marry the future Dauphin of France. No more would the Royal Armies of Scotland and England face each other on the fields of war, but that did not mean the end of attack. Mary de Guise, the Queen Mother, died two years later, her mission complete, and was interred at St. Pierre de Rheims Cathedral in her native France.

*T*he 1558 invasion of the town was a little different in the sense, a peace treaty had been agreed some years earlier at Berwick but that did not deter the Wardens of the northern counties of England, which included Henry Percy, 9th Earl of Northumberland, who still found the need to cross the border and destroy anything which lay in their path. The people of Duns, once more, suffered and lost so much including countless friends and loved ones but they never lost their dignity nor the will to carry on. What they did lose though, as we have seen, was their cherished town records, all destroyed during the constant burnings of the town.

*D*uring all the trauma of attack and counter attack, there was some good news for the Dingers of Duns, their beloved town was created the County Town of Berwickshire, Though that title would swing back and forth between Duns and Greenlaw several times over the centuries, for that moment at least, it created an even larger sense of pride and well being amongst the populace knowing they now lived in the most important town in the shire.

*F*rom the closing stages of the 15th and the greater part of the 16th century, the English for varying reasons, wreaked havoc on the Scots and the total roll of casualties will never be known. They showed, that the Auld Alliance of Scotland and France, was no match for their military might but yet, Scotland survived. What the English did help change in Scotland, was the Scots' beliefs and continuing adherence of the Church of Rome. Indeed, in 1547, and the last of Seymour's (Duke of Somerset) attacks, the English brought with them many new bibles and anti-Papacy propaganda, literature which was liberally given to the many. While the seeds had already been sown in Scotland and two major figures in the fight for reform, Patrick Hamilton and Andrew Wishart had already been executed for their beliefs, others loomed large, particularly John Knox.

Right : Statue of John Knox on the Knox Institute building, original Knox Academy in Haddington. The school was the first modern descendant of medieval Haddington Grammar, a Franciscan establishment and one of the oldest schools in the world.

~ A New Beginning ~
~ New Town, New Religion, New Threat ~

After, at least two thousand years, the old fort on the hill and its descendants had gone forever. From the coming of the peaceful Gudoddin and relatively peaceful Romans, to the warlike Angles, Saxons, Danes, Northumbrians and English, the people were left with nought. The people of the old town were a proud, hardy race with no intentions of being dispersed in the countryside, though a few did, meaning the pace of rebuilding increased as never before. Soon the new town of Dunse was under way leaving the old Burnt Town consigned to the past forever, though the fortitude of its inhabitants would never allow their proud heritage to die with their old town, a pride borne of stubbornness, which has survived to the present day,

With the church already in place, probably from the first half of the 12th century, and the castle in situ no later than the 14th century, possibly before, it is almost certain, in common sense terms, there would be a form of thoroughfare, a row of houses perhaps, betwixt the two. That thoroughfare, now known as Castle Street, would probably lead virtually all the way between the two major establishments in the town, the castle and church which is said to have stood slightly to the north of the present kirk in an area which now houses a section of the Square. While some buildings had been built to the south of the old town in earlier times, in the wake of Henry VIII's sorties, many more buildings were being constructed forming the beginning of a new town.

After the attack of 1558 however, building work was renewed at pace and, while old Teindhillgreen, Castle Wynd and Spinning Yard Head had already been built, what better way to expand south than by naming the first new major street, The New Town?

An old plate of Newtown Street in much of its current form. Looking from near the Horse Market section in the west to the houses at the far end which were then part of Castle Street - Courtesy of Ronald Morrison & Dunse History Socirty

~ *A New Beginning* ~

*W*e must remind ourselves though, this was not simply about building a few new homes for the homeless, it was about building an entirely new town virtually from scratch with all the required elements within. The church was, of course, a very important part of the lives of everyone in the community and it really is quite surprising the holy building was not laid completely bare in the vile attacks which destroyed the town but it is certain, it would be damaged but to what degree we don't know since all the records were destroyed. The day would come though, when the old kirk became unfit for purpose but it did survive until the late 18th century before a new one, almost certainly the third church in Duns, was built, slightly to the south.

*F*ollowing on from the New Town, a new link was built between that street and Spinning Yard Head, known as Meetinghouse Wynd then on to the south when the first buildings of Willis Wynd, Market Wynd and what became known as Black Bull Wynd, were constructed. A form of market square would then be formed with other thoroughfares to and from heading in all directions. Fore Street led out to the west to join with the Langton Gate as did Back Street which formed a slightly alternative route to Langton Gate before Shambles Wynd was constructed leading to the south as was Church Lane and finally the Easter Gate which crossed another thoroughfare which later became known as Bank Street, a street which, with Shambles Wynd, led towards Bridgend and the Coldstream Gate. Another street leading from Castle Wynd to the east, was known as Back o' the Manse. While homes for the people were the principal purpose, so many businesses moved in, many of which were conducted from the peoples' front rooms before being converted to what we now know as shops. Fore Street and Shambles Wynd became, in time, the busiest of the business thoroughfares. It has to be emphasised though, that while the building of the new town emanated from the 16th century, the most southerly reaches were not completed until the latter part of the 18th century.

South Street, formerly Fore Street
Courtesy of Dunse History Society

~ *A New Beginning* ~

That is not to say the buildings we now see are from that period, since so much renewal has taken place over time, right up to the present day and so many of the fine buildings we now see, replaced older buildings in the 19th century.

Another important occasion of the 16th century, which we have already touched on, and one of the most profound changes in Scotland's history, was the coming of the reformed religion. Preaching Catholicism was banned as the Calvinist doctrine was followed according to John Knox's First Book of Discipline. In time, the new Church of Scotland accepted Melville's Second Book of Discipline and that book of Presbyterian code is still with us today. That did not please everyone but most, particularly the working classes, were content with the great shift in the stance of the church. It has to be said, being a Catholic was never made a criminal offence in itself but the preaching and promotion was banned in the greater degree though Catholicism did survive throughout the years, albeit 'underground'. It all took time to educate and employ ministers for the new church but many Catholic priests reformed and preached in some churches while readers conducted the service in many others. Because all the great houses of education were in the south of the country, fully ordained ministers arrived there earlier, before moving across the country with the Highlands and Islands bringing up the rear. In the case of Collegiate Churches, which were patronised by rich landowners, preachers appeared to be allowed to stay longer and this was, apparently, the case during the early years of the Reformation at Dunbar Church and its prebends, including Duns.

At the Reformation, Mary of Scots was the reigning monarch but her principal interest in Berwickshire was to take steps to curb the lawlessness of the Border Reivers. In 1566, she undertook a tour ot the Eastern Borders which included visits to Kelso, Hume, Langton, Duns, Wedderburn, Chirnside and Eyemouth but it would take her son, James, who visited the region on more than one occasion, to finally come to terms with that particular problem. It seems the king, during his visit to Duns in 1602, discussed the troublesome situation which forever threatened the peace of the two nations and may have attended church during that visit since he did mention the church as the *Prebendaria de Dunse* and the 'Mother Church' as his *Ecclessia de Sancti Bac de Dunbar*. While the reivers were still free to wander the streets of Duns, the king, after his ascension to the throne of England a year later, used the stronger arms of his new position to, more or less, put an end to their cross border violence, of burning, of theft and, worst of all, of...murder.

On the subject of Queen Mary, every year, the Marie Stuart Society perform an act of remembrance at the her tomb in Westminster Abbey and, in December 2014, a Duns lady, Marianne Morrison, had the proud honour of dedication and the laying of a floral tribute to the much lamented Queen of Scots, arguably the most famous woman in history, and the most mistreated.

~ *A New Beginning* ~

People do forget though, as a child, Mary left a Catholic country, Scotland, to go to another Catholic country, France. She lived her life as a Catholic but when she returned to post Reformation Scotland, she was in a daze, but she did rule with some dignity though at times, it appeared, she made some poor decisions with the company she kept. She was executed on 8th February at Fotheringay Castle, after a dubious trial ordered by Elizabeth I of England before being interred at Peterborough Cathedral but her body was exhumed on the orders of her son, James VI and re-interred in Westminster Abbey.

Following the Union of the Crowns in 1603, it was reasonable to believe, attacking armies from the south were over, well they were over as already mentioned but that cessation only applied to the Royal armies. There was more trouble on the horizon with several wars still to be dealt with.

Scotland's principal concern was the Stuart kings' attempts to force the Episcopacy on the people of Scotland, where the Reformed Church was still very much in its infancy. King James did make efforts to reform the Scottish Church but, from 1637, Charles I attempted to force a new English prayer book and a bishopric on the Scots, an attempt which was fiercely resisted by the people. That scenario was enacted for many decades at the behest of Scotland's own Royals, right up to the moment the dithering James VII fled the country for France.

In August of 1639, the Confession of Faith of the Kirk of Scotland, better known as the National Covenant, was declared and soon to be sternly defended against the stupidity of the Stuart kings in London. Many thousands signed the Covenant including a copy of which, dating from 1639, is retained in Duns Castle to the present day. The Covenant was a direct result of the English Liturgy being preached at the High Kirk of St. Giles a year earlier, a sermon which caused serious rioting not only in Edinburgh but across the nation. There was bitter interchanging of alliances during the so called Bishops' Wars, the War of the Three Kingdoms, the English Civil Wars, the signing of the Solemn League and Covenant, (an alliance with Cromwell) the re-engagement with the king, Cromwell's thinly disguised occupation of Scotland and so on. So much of that affected the Borders, particularly Duns, when General Alexander Leslie assembled a huge Covenanting army at Duns Law in readiness to engage forces of Charles I who were based at Berwick. The king was attempting, through force, to push his new Episcopal doctrine down the throat of the Scottish Church. Leslie, though using Duns Castle as his headquarters, built fortifications on the Law in the case of a surprise attack but was more interested in making ready to meet the king's army head on.

The action ultimately ended in a stand off, and the two sides agreed a truce before the signing of the Pacification of Berwick took place. While the truce ended the first War of the Bishops, it was no more than a means of allowing Charles more time to strengthen his army before recommencing hostilities. If

~ A New Beginning ~

nothing else, the Covenanting soldiers of Scotland had laid down their mantle in defence of their church and on that day, 18th of June, 1639, they were said to have stated *"Scotland retained her religious freedom, not by Canon Law, nor by Civil Law but by Duns Law"* - a phrase which has gone down in the annals of both national and church history.

Only a year later, in 1640, the king ordered his troops to attack the garrison on the Law in an attempt to seize Leslie's impressive array of cannon but the Royalists were soundly repelled and sent packing on their way back south.

Troops were then billeted along the border, including a strong force on the Law in readiness, in the case of another attempt by the king, which did indeed arrive the following year as we have seen. This time however, the Covenanters were in full readiness, and, after the skirmish in Duns, crossed the border and took the Royalist army full on. The Battle of Newburn in 1640 saw the king abandoning Newcastle and beating a retreat to Ripon where another document of cessation was signed but that wasn't the end by any means, that simply put an end, finally, to the Bishops' Wars. The rest, as we have already seen, was still to come, yet more bloody business lay ahead.

This stone, within a timber fenced enclosure and protected by a metal grid, is where a Scottish Army under General Leslie reputedly raised the standard of the National Covenant in 1639. The cairn behind has a plaque which is inscribed:

THIS CAIRN COMMEMORATES THE ENCAMPMENT HERE OF THE COVENANTERS UNDER GENERAL ALEXANDER LESLIE IN 1639

Courtesy of Walter Baxter

The wars ultimately did put an end to the life of the king, Charles I, who was executed at the Palace of Whitehall in 1649 by the Parliamentarians. That however, did not dissuade the next two Stuart Kings from making the same mistakes.

Oliver Cromwell and his trusty 'Guardian of Scotland', General George Monck, were no shrinking violets and they and their troops caused so much damage and carried out so much theft from the Scottish State and the people of

~ *A New Beginning* ~

Scotland, including emptying the banks of all their reserves and Duns did not escape their attentions. Soon after the second Battle of Dunbar in 1650, his troops were in need of so much and Dunse was chosen to 'agree' to supply the army with food, clothing and shoes, it is even reported the English *'New Model Army'* drank the towns' breweries dry. There was a garrison in the town for some years but in fairness, there was no bloodshed and what troops were in Dunse were said, not to be an army of occupation but as 'billeted soldiers of the Commonwealth"

The same General Monck was the man who mustered his brigade of English veterans at Coldstream, in readiness to march on London. On 1st January, 1660, the Lord General's Regiment of Foot set off on their epic march, a march which led to the Restoration of the monarchy in the form of Charles II who had already been crowned King of Scots in 1649. His brother, James II & VII became king on Charles' death in 1685 but he too, had not learned his lessons and was deposed only three years later when he fled to France. Monck's regiment were named the Coldstream Foot Guards in 1670 before in 1855 becoming the Coldstream Guards, a proud regiment indeed.

The uncertainty of the Kirk remained in doubt until 1688 and the Glorious Revolution in England, when Mary, daughter of James II & VII, and her husband, William, Prince of Orange, were invited to take the throne. While the Presbyterian Church remained the National Church of Scotland, the Episcopal movement gained ground and was ultimately accepted within the Scottish community particularly, at first, among the aristocracy, but the church has grown dramatically over the centuries. The Catholic Church, of course, has been re-established in Scotland in more recent times but more of that later.

1688, brought the beginning of the end to a sad era which sullied the proud boast of Scots, that their own Royal House, had ascended the throne of first England, and later, Ireland. James VI as we have seen, was the first to make some efforts to introduce bishoprics to the country of his birth before his son, and his grandsons followed in his footsteps. While the house survived through Queens Mary and Anne, the writing was already on the wall. If only the House of Stewart (Stuart) had adhered to Robert the Bruce's words to his people after his coronation in 1306, "I am here to serve you, the people" and not dwelt on their own arrogant self belief of their *'Divine Right of Kings'*, they could still have been on the throne of the United Kingdom in the present day.

Two very important local 'happenings' took place in the latter part of the 17th century; first of all in 1670, when the Cockburn family purchased the Barony of Duns then in 1696 when John Hay, 1st Marquis of Tweeddale and Lord Chancellor of Scotland bought the estates for his son, Lord William Hay soon after William's marriage to Elizabeth Seton. The present Hay family of Duns Castle are of the 'Duns and Drumelzier' branch of the family and are, apart from Royal descent already mentioned, descended from three of the

~ A New Beginning ~

most noble families who, in their own way, enlightened early Scotland, the Hays, the Setons and the de Giffards.

Another note of a more than passing interest during the 17th century, was the case of Margaret Lumsden, a young woman of the town, who was charged with demonic behaviour and removed to Canongate Tolbooth in Edinburgh, for questioning by Maitland, the Earl of Lauderdale. Later in 1630, her whole family were incarcerated beside her for further questioning by the Privy Council. No actual proof of her being a witch was ever produced but one day, a minister spoke to Margaret, an uneducated girl, in Latin, and to his astonishment, she replied in better Latin than the good man had used when speaking to her. Of course that emanated from the obsessive witch hunts ordered by the late king, James VI after a ship carrying his queen-to-be, Anne of Denmark, was driven on to rocks off North Berwick by a great storm of 1590, which the king blamed on a coven of witches who were said to be practising their unholy rites near the auld kirk on Anchor Green at North Berwick; that provoked the infamous witch hunts.

The incomparable Reverend Thomas Boston was born in Duns in 1676 and his memory has lived long and true in Scottish Church History. In the street where he was born, the New Town, there exists his place of birth and the school building which bore his name as did, to the south of the Public Park, the Boston Free Kirk once stood. Thomas Boston is one of Duns' greatest sons and one of the best remembered of all the pioneering ministers. His work, *Human Nature in its Fourfold State,* one of the most important writings of the 18th century, is still a much revered work. Thomas was born the son of John Boston and Alison Trotter in 1676 and died at Ettrick and was buried in that kirkyard where he preached for many years having been translated from Simprim Kirk in 1707. He was a school teacher, philosopher and, of course one of the great ministers and church leaders in his country's history.

Rev. Thomas Boston
Dunse History Society
Website

In 1689, what many perceive as *Duns' Own,* The King's Own Scottish Borderers was raised and, within weeks, were called in to action at the Battle of Killiecrankie and though the anti-Jacobite army (including the KOSB) was defeated, in the following days the regiment defended Dunkeld 'with great gusto' and saved the town from being ravaged by the angry Highlanders. This was the beginning of a noble, proud and courageous regiment, a regiment which many men of Duns joined and died for. As we shall see later, the Duns reserve militia were part of the great regiment, a regiment which was eventually granted the freedom of Duns.

~ *A New Beginning* ~

*F*rom that point, Killiecrankie and Dunkeld, the 'KOSB', then known as Semphill's Regiment, was involved in nearly every British action, including their efforts in thwarting the 1715 and 1745 Jacobite Rebellions, when they were part of Cumberland's victorious 'redcoat' army at Culloden while they were known as the 25th (Sussex) Regiment of Foot. Their final, and glorious title of the King's Own Scottish Borderers, was accorded them in 1805. Their list of Battle Honours is impressive and stretches from the Namur in 1695, Minden in 1709 then through every major conflict which the British Army was involved in right up to the Gulf War in 1991. So many Dingers served in the KOSB over the centuries and like many of their fellow townsmen, died for the safety and peace of their beloved town and country. The regiment was amalgamated with the Royal Scots in 2006 to form the Royal Scots Borderers which is now the 1st Battalion of the Royal Regiment of Scotland. Interestingly, during the 1715 Jacobite uprising, General Mackintosh's Highland militia visited Duns but it is not clear what, if any, damage was incurred. There was also thought to be a Highland platoon which drove their way through Duns in 1745 demanding food while heading south-east soon after ordering new boots for every man, at the town of Selkirk.

*B*efore we leave the 18th century, it is important to mention more of the notable events of the 1700s. The magnificent Pavilion Lodge entrance to Duns Castle was built in 1770, the old kirk was demolished and rebuilt in 1790 but not before the memorable visit of Scotland's National Bard, Robert Burns in 1787 but more of that in due course. Around the same time, roads were being improved thanks to the Turnpike Trust. Toll bars and houses were built everywhere including no less than seven around Duns with two being situated within the town. The population at large, were not keen to pay tolls as they travelled the countryside, even though the monies did improve the thoroughfares. Within months, two country tolls were destroyed by fire before the tolls situated in the town itself were laid bare. In 1792, a sparkling new Market Cross, the present Cross, was erected in the square, yet another joyful sign of the town's status personified amidst great celebrations.

*B*uilding works on the town were resumed at pace during the 18th and into the 19th centuries as the new town was, more than ever, beginning to take shape. The new town layout, though built from the late 16th century onwards, was a tried and trusted style of the times with all roads leading to a town square. North Street and South Street parting company towards the west of the square to meet again in the centre of town, at the town house, just beyond Golden Square then on to Easter Street. It is a layout emanating from late Scottish medieval times and which can be witnessed in many old towns nearby including Kelso, Lauder and Haddington. The principal building in the town was the tolbooth which, for centuries, held the town's miscreants. It would almost appear as if that tolbooth was situated thus, as a form of "no matter

~ *A New Beginning* ~

what direction you enter town, step out of line and I am here, waiting for you" Of course building work was ongoing and most of the buildings we now see were built from the 19th century, though there is a building with much 17th century fabric within, in Newtown Street. That brings us to a glossary of the street names and an explanation for names used earlier in this study.

The north side of Castle Street was once known as Teindhillgreen while the bottom section which leads on to Market Square was Castle Wynd; the square itself was known as Market Place. The Teindhillgreen we now know was known as Back o' the Manse, Clouds was Spinning Yard Head, while Gourlay's Wynd was then called Meetinghouse Wynd. Here is a list of the rest.

Present title	Old title
Blackbull Street	Black Bull Wynd
Langtongate	The Langton Gate
North Street	Back Street
South Street	Fore Street
Currie Street	Bank Street
Easter Street	The Easter Gate
Murray Street	Shambles Wynd

Others not mentioned have remained the same over the centuries.

The north section of Castle Street which was known as Teind Hill Green in days gone by. The building on the middle right, is the present day no.1 Teindhillgreen, which was once the Ewe and Lamb Inn, so appropriate since it was situated in the middle of the old sheep market. The original Teind Hill Green stretched up this route and was the site of the old Teind Barn where local farmers contributed a teind (tenth part) of their crop to the minister of the parish.
Photo courtesy of Dunse History Society

~ *A New Beginning* ~

The present layout of the town centre has remained the same for two centuries, apart from the street names and, if a Dinger from the latter part of the 18th century was able to return, they would recognise their town though perhaps not all of the present buildings.

A new tolbooth **(right)** was built in the square in 1680 by the Cockburn family of Langton and Duns; the building contained meeting rooms and offices for the Burgesses, the domain of the Bailiffs and the town gaol, where they 'looked after' the town's wrong doers. Interestingly, another gaol was built in later times, near the site of the Episcopal Church, Christ Church. In 1795 the tolbooth was destroyed by fire before being rebuilt in the early 19th century as a town house for the Cockburns and can still be seen today on the corner of Market Square and South Street. In 1976, a clock on the upper section of the building was presented by the Rotary Club of Duns while, in 1990, Princess Margaret unveiled a plaque on the building commemorating the 500th anniversary of the town's elevation to Burgh of Barony. In 1820, a sparkling new Town Hall, of the highest order, was built, financed, in part, by the Hay family and opened by Alexander Chrystie of Grueldykes. Sadly that building had to be demolished in 1966 having spent some years as a factory for Robert Pringle and Son Ltd. The old town house was originally topped by a spire but the spire was removed for safety purposes leaving the beautifully

DUNS TOLBOOTH 1680

The Town Hall, or Market House – Courtesy of Dunse History Society

~ *A New Beginning* ~

adorned pinnacles at each corner of the tower. On the day of dedication and opening of the new building, many Freemason Lodges of Berwickshire attended the service conducted by the Rev. Robert Cunningham. When the opening ceremony to the great James Gillespie masterpiece was over, the Brotherhood and their guests marched to the Black Bull Inn for more speeches and a celebratory dinner. Sadly, at the opening of the Town House in the Square, the Market Cross was removed not to be seen again until 1897 and Queen Victoria's Diamond Jubilee when the famous structure was erected in the Public Park. Finally it was returned to the Square on its present spot, in 1994 and remains on that spot to the present day, a true symbol of the Burgh's proud status. All the streets which kept the town in touch with the outside world, Langtongate, Back o' the Manse, Easter Gate and Bridgend all contained, and still do, so many inspiring and beautiful houses, another sign of the town's growing importance...and prosperity. With the arrival of banks including the Bank of Scotland, the Linen Bank, The Royal Bank and the Bank of Glasgow, law firms and local authority departments. The town began to spread to the south and east as more and more businessmen relocated to a place of growing importance.

The Mercat Cross

The 19th century saw the town, perhaps at the peak of its growth in terms of business, travel and commerce. The railway arrived, first to Reston on the main East Coast Line then later heading west to St. Boswells, Earlston and beyond, giving access to the old Waverley line. There were sparkling new rail stations, not just at Duns but at Earlston, Gordon, Greenlaw, Marchmont, Edrom and Chirnside.

Duns Railway Station courtesy of Ronald Morrison

~ *A New Beginning* ~

A look at a directory of 1837 gives us a better idea of the make up of the town's businesses, the list I must say is long but important to note: Seven bakers' shops, seventeen grocers, many of whom supplied ales and spirits, three hairdressers, three ironmongers, one of whom also sold jewellery, five tailors, four dressmakers and milliners, seven linen and woollen drapers, seven butchers' shops, two tobacco manufacturers, 'several' clockmakers, the town's most renowned product, 15 vitners, nine of whom were in the licensed inns of Horseshoe Inn, the Hammermen's, the King's Arms, the Thistle, the Ordnance Arms, the Plough, Cross Keys, the Britannia and the Ewe and Lamb. That total does not include the old posting inns of the Black Bull and White Swan or the other inn on the Newtown, the Hunt. In time, the Dunlop Trust Hotel on a corner site in South Street was opened as a temperance house, meaning there was no consumption of alcohol allowed. Let us not forget either, the house at 2, Newtown Street which was a tippling inn before becoming the Horn Inn. There were also 19 shoemakers, three book sellers and printers, three breweries, five cabinet makers, lawyers, sheriff's office, police, tax and excise office and several of every other trade known to man. There also was a woollen mill, a tannery and a large bleachfield. Another mill which was reputed to have made a material known as Clud, a yard of which was purchased by Robert Burns during his visit. The clud factory was sited at what was then known as Spinning Yard Head. The post office can be added to the list as could a daily coach service to Edinburgh which left the square every day at 8am. Other works were provided by a nearby rope works and paper mills, fresh water works, quarries and several farms. Then there were the auctioneers for the markets and it would seem no one was unemployed and, if they were, there was a poorhouse with workhouse if required, for the elderly, sick and unemployed. Some people frown on the thought of poor houses but really, that was another very benevolent act of the town fathers in what was essentially an early form of welfare system. In the poorhouses, those who were fit and able, were found jobs, mainly employed in keeping the town clean, neighbouring mills or on local farms.

*W*e have already indicated, the street where most of the local retail business was located was Shambles Wynd perhaps the busiest but there were shops in all the streets. New Town was where most of the farm animal trading took place as did so many of the other markets. Soon, the the press arrived when the Berwickshire News was founded the town in 1869 and still provides a quality newspaper to the present day though now based in Berwick.

*T*here were several churches which are no longer with us including the Boston Memorial Church which was built in 1838 as a Quoad Sacra kirk but joined the Free Kirk Movement at the schism of 1843. It later became part of the United Presbyterian Church but at the re-unification of 1929, rejoined the Church of Scotland but closed in 1953, later to be demolished with housing

~ *A New Beginning* ~

built on the site. Interestingly the Boston Free Kirk was united with the Free Kirk of Langton for seven years from 1927. The great Drumclog Bell, an integral part of the Boston Kirk is now proudly displayed at the entrance to the sheltered housing complex at Boston Court. The East Church in Easter Street began life as a Secession church in 1743, on lands which were purchased from the Hays and, some say, gifted to the congregation by Thomas Trotter of the paper making family, a parish church elder. That congregation converted to the Anti-Burgher movement, later becoming part of UP congregation of churches. When it closed, it lay empty for many years before being converted to a cinema which too, has now departed the scene, burning to the ground in 1966. Then there was the South Kirk, in Currie Street, also part of the UP congregation which was built in 1852 to replace an older Relief Kirk of 1751 but that too has long since closed and is now a carpet warehouse. Clouds was the location of the West Burgher Kirk, the congregation of which had split from the East Secession Church in Easter Street, which, as we know, joined the Anti-Burgher faction. Other churches which were founded during the 19th century were the Scottish Episcopal Church in Teindhillgreen which was founded in 1854 and the Roman Catholic Church was founded in 1860 though the present church building was not erected until 1883. There is also a mortuary chapel at Knoll and a few, long closed meeting halls including the Faith Mission in South Street which moved to Willis Wynd but has closed in recent times while another former chapel in Willis Wynd can still be seen though not now in ecclesiastical use. As we have seen, to the north, at Birkensyde, now known as Chapel, stood the St. Mary Magdalene Church which contained a hospital which was referred to as the Duns Poorhouse in the 14th century but that establishment and its graveyard have long since disappeared the scene, buried under centuries of farming. Other denominations at Duns were the Brethern who were active for over 100 years in premises at the Square and a group of Methodists who worshipped in various houses near the end of the 18th and early 19th centuries. We shall read more in to the present day churches in later pages.

The town also contained a remarkable ten schools including the parish and infants' schools which originated in what became the Parish Church Halls. The Boston Free Kirk School on Newtown Street **(left, courtesy of Graham Robson)** was well attended but the rest were made up of mainly one teacher, day schools for boarders and would probably be privately funded including Wellfield Academy at the top of Easter Street.

~ *A New Beginning* ~

Duns boasted one of the earliest fire stations in the country when it opened in the New Town in 1806, Other important buildings in Newtown Street which were built during the 19th century, were the county buildings, the police station and the Sheriff Courthouse, banks, schools, police station and the Corn Exchange. Perhaps Newtown Street's most important development of the 19th century was the opening of the Berwickshire High School in 1896. Children from all over the sprawling county attended the school if they had passed their qualifying examination at the Primary stage. Many of those children were unable to travel daily in those early times but the solution was found at Southfield House where they were lodged Monday to Friday each week.

The railway, as we have seen, arrived in 1859 but, sadly it all came to an end and while some freight activity continued, the line finally closed in 1965.

The fact the town had no immediate source of water did not mean the people went without though sometimes the water had to be carried a fair distance. In 1747 however, a source of fresh spring water was discovered just to the south in the lands of Nisbet House, Nisbet Rhodes and Duns Mill. The obvious benefits the spa brought to the everyday lives of the local people was clear but many travelled from afar believing the waters were beneficial to their health. At one stage, the town fathers had thoughts of Duns becoming a Tonbridge Wells or, at least, a St. Ronans, but the principal benefit was to the general health of local people. The very mention of Nisbet House brings to mind two battles which were fought in that vicinity but we shall discuss the two conflicts a little later.

In 1882, after a meeting in the town house, the town's name was returned to Duns, which was described at that time, as its ancient name, and the name it retains in the present day. It must be said, many local people do believe, Dunse was the original name.

Old Langtongate with the Volunteer Hall on the right
Courtesy of Dunse History Society

Many groups and societies were created in Duns but perhaps, the most important was the local militia (as we have seen) the Dunse detachment of the 2nd (Berwickshire) Volunteer Battalion, King's Own Scottish Borderers, a

~ *A New Beginning* ~

regiment so close to the hearts of all Dingers. Of course a militia would have been formed from early times but that would be in the hands of the local laird, more especially before the Treaty of Union in 1707. The local detachment did most of their training and drilling in the the Volunteer Hall but towards the end of the 19th century, the hall was becoming unfit for purpose meaning a new centre became an urgent priority. Thanks to the generosity of the public at large and to General Charles Hope, Commanding Officer of the battalion, the hall was completed and opened by the good general himself in 1895.

*T*he Volunteer Hall is simply another of the many wonderful buildings in a town full of fine architecture and it is not difficult to find. On every street corner, in every street, wynd or alley, beauty and antiquity awaits us all.

*O*nly a few years before the building of the Volunteer Hall, in 1892, money was provided by Andrew Smith of Whitchester, to buy land for the creation of a park for public use, a place of recreation, fun and peace. Of course that park still provides all it was meant to do and every man, woman or child who lived in the town since that time have but happy memories of a cherished place of peace. A place where dads met, wives 'gossiped' and bairns had the time of their young lives.

*A*s witnessed, from the latter part of the 16th century to present day, the town grew at pace. The fact it was, off and on the County Town, a title shared over the centuries with Greenlaw, meant it attracted so many to the town, knowing gainful employment was to be had. Of course more housing had to be built and it was, but the more affordable social housing had to wait, like every other community in Scotland, until the 20th century.

*B*efore looking at the town of today, Let us take a walk along memory lane and have a look at some old prints of the town as it developed over the years.

Looking west on Newtown Street

~ Old Photographs ~

Market Place East

Looking east on The Langton Gate.

Notice the building in the middle which is no longer there

Currie Street prior to widening. Notice the South Church, now a carpet warehouse

~ *Old Photographs* ~

The Market Place north

East end of Newtown Street as it 'junctions' at Castle Street. The building at the end of the street was removed to allow Newtown Street to go further and bend in to Currie Street forming a bypass to the town centre

Left : A view of old Easter Street

All photographs on these pages, courtesy of
Ronald Morrison
and the Dunse History Society

~ *Old Photographs* ~

The foot of Bridgend

Cattle market on the site of Aitchison's Garage
at the junction of Bridgend,
Currie Street and Murray Street

~ *Today's Town* ~

Before looking at the town of today, we must remember the men of Duns and district who gave their lives in so many wars since the Treaty of Union in 1707. There has been trouble somewhere in the world in virtually every decade since and the young men of Duns joined the lads from every corner of the United Kingdom to fight all across the globe. The wars which have affected the community most recently are, of course the two World Wars of the 20th century. So many young men died and we thought those were the wars to end all wars but not a bit of it. Most recently, British troops have been brought home from Afghanistan where so many more died and, as always, we all pray for peace in the world but there seems no end in sight.

Above :
Duns War Memorial

Left :
Polish War Memorial

Apart from the Parish War Memorial, there is another in the park, in remembrance of Polish troops billeted around Duns who also gave their lives in their quest for freedom. The 2nd and 3rd Armoured Divisions of the Polish Army carried out their training around the town before leaving to join their British counterparts in the war against Germany but, sadly 127 men never came back. What did arrive back in Berwickshire with the Polish Troops was a Syrian Brown Bear which the soldiers dubbed Wojtek. The young bear was given the rank of private and joined in by helping move heavy objects during manoeuvres. Not only did he work as a soldier, he also loved a pint of ale. In 1947 Wojtek was gifted to Edinburgh Zoo where he lived the rest of his life before dying in December 1963 at the age of 21. There are memorials to the remarkable animal in the War museum in London and in Quebec, Canada and there are moves afoot to present the town of Duns with a full size model of the brave soldier, Private Wojtek. In recent times, Duns has been twinned with, and cemented relations with the town of Żagań in Western Poland.

~ Today's Town ~

*O*f course, there are so many changes in the modern day and not all for the better, though better roads is one plus, providing easier communications though, as we know, no longer a railway. Much better education for the children, probably the greatest...and most important change of all, was now well and truly established with the new High School the pride of the town. Other areas which have improved beyond recognition throughout the 20th and 21st centuries, are healthcare which included the now closed Whitchester Cottage and the current Knoll Hospitals along with better ophthalmic and dentistry services. Perhaps the best way to describe the town of the modern day is to take a leisurely walk along the A6105 road from near to the junction with Gavinton.

*O*n our way we cross the Langton Bridge over the burn of the same name, when Langton Estate's most majestic lodge house comes in to view sitting proud at an entrance on the bend. Soon the main entrance to Langton looms large, guarded by another lodge and an architecturally supreme gateway. A full description of the majestic but much lamented house can be witnessed in the *Great Houses* section. On past Scotstoun and Pouterlynie where once existed a thriving weaving industry, including linen manufacture where many of the weavers were of Flemish origin. Just beyond is Hardens Park, former home of Duns Rugby Football Club which was founded in 1878 and currently plays in the BT National League Division I, a sad fall from grace for a club competing for a place in the Premiership only a few years ago. The rugby club now plays on a new pitch at the old high school near a state of the art, swimming complex in the company of so many other fitness and sporting facilities including that of Duns Football Club who ply their trade in the East of Scotland League. The club was founded in 1882, one of the oldest in the southern reaches of Eastern Scotland and, during their long 'career' have won no fewer than 18 cups, a remarkable record. Near the old rugby pitch is Duns Golf Course where one of the oldest golf clubs in the Borders still look for birdies and eagles. Duns Golf Club was established in 1894 and benefits from a fine course, with a par of 70, on the lower slopes of Hardens Hill. At the end of a successful, or not so successful, shift on the golf course, the players have the benefit of a fine clubhouse to relax before their journey home and telling friends of the 'two inch' putt they missed to win the match. A bit like the local anglers and their three feet long monsters which 'got away'.

*N*ext is the old hamlet of Clockmill, and the site of some magnificent homes, situated just yards to the west of the new Berwickshire High School. Before going further, it must be said...again, there is such a wonderful array of very fine houses in the town, some verging on mansion status. The new school is housed in a magnificent new building of 2009 and sitting directly opposite the previous high school which had served the town since 1957. Those schools, on Langtongate, are the descendants of the original school which

~ *Today's Town* ~

opened on Newtown Street, amidst great rejoicing, in the late 19th century. Of course the high school was not the first school in the town as we shall see, but it did give every child of the entire county, the opportunity of higher education. At present the old high school is under going major re-development. To the south of the schools, across the Earl's Meadow, is Grueldykes, the home of the old de Duns family then, in much later times the very benevolent Chrystie family. On past the most imposing entrance gateway known as *Sally's Lodge,* the main entrance to Duns Castle, complete with towers, archway and a small belfry. Soon we pass the old primary school, the town's oldest school building still being used though plans are afoot to remove to the old high school building at Langtongate in the near future.

Now we have reached Newtown Street, a street which is home to so many fine buildings some of which of course, we have already mentioned. Like the former Bank of Scotland and British Linen bank buildings, the police station, Sheriff Court and the Horn Inn.

Left : The County Library

Below: Berwickshire High School, the third high school in Duns.
Courtesy of Jim Barton, Geograph

There is also the library which is the second library building in the town but it is to no. 44 we now look. That house is home to a museum, the Jim Clark Room, dedicated to the life and times of the late, great, world champion racing driver who died at Hockenheim, Germany in 1968. The free-to-enter venue, which contains much of his memorabilia and trophies, is a must see venue when in the town.

~ *Today's Town* ~

*B*orn in Fife and buried at Chirnside Kirkyard, Jim lived and grew up near Chirnside and, of course, was a well known face around the town. He enjoyed a sparkling career, in touring cars, rally cars and, of course, Formula One - he even won the world famous Indianapolis 500 in 1965. During his Formula One career, Jim triumphed in no less than 25 Grand Prix races and won poll position on an amazing 33 occasions on the way to winning the World Championship twice. He held every record in the sport and is still regarded by experts, as the greatest Formula One driver of all time. His death marked the end of an exceptional era in his sport and the career of one of the nicest, most approachable people in the world of sport...and in the streets of Duns.

*I*n May, 2015, a great display was put on, to mark the 50th anniversary of the great man winning The Formula One, Formula Two and the Tasman Championships as well as the Indianapolis 500 race, all in the same year, 1965. That event attracted many well known faces from the world of of motor sport including another of Scotland's racing greats, Jackie Stewart. *T*he event, organised by Club Lotus and the Jim Clark Trust, attracted hundreds of enthusiasts, all eager to be part of such an unique occasion and witness the wonderful racing cars on display. Exciting news of the next instalment of the Jim Clark Rally has just been announced and even more spectators are expected to attend the new formula in June of 2016, meaning

Jim Clark Room © Walter Baxter

exciting times ahead, further remembering the great man. The house, which contains the Jim Clark Room, was once a home of the Cockburn family and known, with its coach house and stables, as Westwood House. There are plans underway, and they are exciting plans, to move the Jim Clark Museum, which is part of the Scottish Borders Museum Service, in to a new, state of the art venue. The rest of Newtown Street contains some of the finest architecture in the entire Scottish Borders including, as indicated, the old Sheriff Courthouse **(across left)** and the former British Linen Bank building **(across right)** and so many more as we have seen.

*L*eading from the north side of Newtown Street is Gourlay's Wynd which, as indicated by its old name, Meetinghouse Wynd, contained a religious house

~ *Today's Town* ~

and still boasts two atmospheric terraces enveloping some new housing near the top of the hill. Gourlay's Wynd leads up to Clouds, an ancient street with the most enthralling and diversified group of old detached houses, including the old West Church, another boasting a Gig House (old stable) with every other competing strongly in the beauty stakes. Now head up the northern section of old Castle Street where exists the old teind barn.

The south side of Newtown Street contains several wynds heading south, like Willis Wynd where you can find an old, disused chapel, a now closed Faith Mission and the old bakery. Further to the east is Blackbull Street where the old coaching inn is still open for business and a lay off which contains the 17th century 'Secret House' and lovely Ranamona. Next is Market Wynd where the cattle market once took centre stage but where now stands a large store and the inevitable old, but lovely houses. Finally is the southern section of Castle Street where once a Parliament was held and a king made his triumphant entry in to the town, with 'reiver bashing' on his mind. That brings us to the Square but before the Square let's look nearer to where it all began.

From the square, head up Castle Street heading north beyond the houses and soon the, Pavilion Lodge, an entrance to Duns Castle comes in to view.

That entrance is of one of two major entrances to the castle estate, the other as we have seen, is on Langtongate. The wonderful building of the 18th century, consists of two round, castellated lodges joined by a beautiful Gothic arch embracing the entrance. All the windows of the beautiful construction are of similar Gothic design and overall, the entire building is a tribute to Robert Hay, the laird of the day, the architect, and the local builders. Nearby is a monument marking the spot where John Duns Scotus was said to have been born, now we have reached one of the town's major attractions, The Duns Castle Reserve, part of the Scottish Wildlife Trust.

~ *Today's Town* ~

Duns Castle Nature Reserve is where a place of history, a place of peace, a place of beauty, peace and tranquility awaits...a place the invading English attempted to destroy forever. We have already seen the history of the Law but there is much more to life than history and sometimes a walk in the haven of a beautiful environ is more important and there are so many beautiful and well used paths on the Reserve. Whether you are looking for all kinds of waterfowl, exotic butterflies, the wonderful water lilies and so many varieties of other wild flowers or the amazing array of trees, you will not be disappointed, no matter which path you choose.

Turning along the path to the right, we pass a marker to the site of the venue for the old Dunse Curling Club before we reach the Hen Poo Loch and the Mill Pond beyond, near where the original Duns Reservoir was situated and where an old sawmill once existed. So many places of natural peace and beauty below the Law, along the ponds, or amidst atmospheric woodland, time is never wasted at such a heavenly location, and though part of the Castle Estate, it is a free to use facility. A view across the Hen Poo, to the left, gives us our first sight of the beautiful Duns Castle but now it's time to venture through the rest of the town, admire the layout and wonderful array of architecture, but before we take another step, it's important to note, most of what we are about to see, was completed before the end of the 19th century. Virtually every building is a listed building of varying categories, all the residue of the technique and skill of architects and builders of the 18th and 19th centuries.

Above : The Pavilion Lodge
Below : The Hen Poo

~ *Today's Town* ~

A walk now down Castle Street is a stroll through the architectural history of the town before it opens up in to the large Square where the sense of wonderment is quite overcoming. It is a fine, compact town centre, retaining so many of its older buildings with some very impressive ones including the two awesome bank buildings, the Working Men's Institute of 1877, the Whip and Saddle Inn and the old Swan Hotel but pride of place must go to the historic Mercat Cross, symbolising the town's status as a Burgh of Barony.

The town contains many fine shops allowing people to purchase their everyday needs in an idyllic, relaxing environ. There are banks, solicitors, coffee shops, butcher, baker, fishmonger, general stores, supermarket, photography, newsagent, sweetie shop, post office and mail sorting depot, gun and game shop, restaurants and takeaways, pharmacy, beauty and hair salons, ironmonger and haberdashery, gift shops, fancy goods, inns and hotels, carpet shops, flower shops, clothing, Veterinary Surgeons...the list goes on and on. While watches and clocks can still be purchased in the town, sadly there are no longer any clock makers for which the town was rightly renowned. Duns of course also contains a fine little hospital and health centre, the Knoll and an excellent community centre at Southfield House on Station Road

Southfield

A grand house of the earlier part of the 19th century which was built for James Curle Robson but is now the Community Centre

North and South Streets which lead off Langtongate, while relatively plain, still retain so many fine buildings as does Golden Square which reaches out from North Street to South Street. The old Dunlop Trust Hotel dominates an open area in South Street, but the old hotel, now a shop with flats overhead has long since gone. Another wonderful building and perhaps the finest in South Street, would you believe? is occupied by, appropriately, an architectural and surveying company. Further along, as mentioned, the Tolbooth House and, directly across, the former Waverley Hotel. Murray Street, the former busy shopping street known as Shambles Wynd, is less busy now but still retains some shops but the lower section, along with Murray Crescent, near the Baillie's Entry, contains some of the finest houses anywhere, including

~ *Today's Town* ~

Marchcroft, Maryfield and the old Barniken Hotel **(below)** which, for many years was a top class hotel, but now lies empty, but that is only some of many.

A Barniken was a fortified house which guarded certain points during violent days and one stood on this site near a causeway. In the earlier part of the 19th century, this beautiful house was built complete with coach houses which were later converted to houses. The big house was later converted to very desirable hotel but has closed in more recent times.

Knoll Hospital and Health Centre, on Station Road, Originally a private home of the latter part of the 19th century, it was converted to a maternity hospital in the 1930s though is now a small general hospital and Duns Health Centre. The hospital was once part of East Lothian Health Board

Like other great houses, Southfield and Barniken, the Knoll too, found a new, worthwhile role as we can see above.

It is difficult not to keep on reiterating the amazing array of great houses, all clustered so close together in every principal thoroughfare, a sight seldom seen in a relatively small rural town. If ever proof was needed of the importance of Duns, it can be seen in all its glory, around every corner. leaving us in little doubt, Duns was indeed a prosperous environ...a town full of confidence and, in a sense that has not changed...Dingers really are upright, forthright and quite simply, lovely folk. They are proud of their town, the centre, the main streets and some of the offshoots too, like Todlaw Road, Bridgend, Teindhillgreen and Trinity Drive for example, where more lovely homes are to be found but that is typical of the whole town including some

~ Today's Town ~

very impressive social housing estates.

Very little remains of the old industries some of which we have already discussed, which included agriculture, quarrying, some weaving, linen manufacture and bleaching fields, a small tannery and a few small breweries but the fact, Duns is the only town in the Borders with no river on its doorstep did not help, as it did others, in the textiles industries though in later years, some textile work did arrive in the town, some of it as we know, in the town hall. There were however, many mills around the town, the most enduring being Duns and Putton Mills to the south and they did contribute greatly to the town's economy. However that does not mean to say the town and district is totally devoid of work.

Most of the local work in recent times however, has been in retail, service, local government and law. There are still important council offices but the Sheriff Court closed in January, 2015. There is an industrial estate on Station Road to the south of the town centre and that too provides some much needed jobs for the local community. The estate contains, a couple of good sized tyre works, garage services, a fish processing plant, garden centres and café, outdoor suppliers, a haulage company, council services, coal company and so much more but most people, if not retired, must commute for work in the present day, either by bus or car since, sadly, as we know, Duns no longer has the added luxury of the railways in this 'modern' age and, while a new 'Borders' railway has recently opened, it is unlikely to be of significant benefit to the Dingers since it terminates at Tweedbank some 26 miles to the west while Berwick Rail Station is just over 15 miles to the east.

The old town is still the local centre for the agricultural industry, a proud role from the beginning and the famous Berwickshire County Show reminds us of that every year. There were busy markets every Wednesday until relatively recent times, when four sheep markets joined three cattle markets held in various parts of the town including North Street, Market Square, Bridgend but principally on Newtown Street. In fact the cattle market survived until very recent times at the foot of Bridgend on the site of Aitchison's garage. One trade which, as we saw earlier, did flourish in Duns was clock making and was famous across the globe. During the 18th and 19th centuries, there were many clockmakers whose works found their way to every corner of the world as their fame grew. Of course there is more to a clock then simply the mechanisms, skilled carpenters were called upon to produce cabinets of the highest quality. There is an interesting article on the Dunse History Society website which contains photographs of Duns clocks some of which are still being found in old chests across the globe, being refurbished and sold for large amounts of money.

The town of today benefits from so many amenities and societies taking care of the townfolks' every need including sport, leisure, care and helping

~ *Today's Town* ~

hands. The amenities and clubs include, Dunse History Society, Southfield Community Centre, the Volunteer Hall, Duns Pipe Band, drama group, archery club, rotary club, mothers' and toddlers' groups, old folks clubs, horticultural society, bowling club, though the curling is no more. Added to that is the Scottish Women's Rural Institute, Church Guilds, Royal Volunteer Service, talking newspaper, angling, disabled riders' group, photographic society, swimming pool and club and of course, the Jim Clark museum. Other club's include a youth centre, girl guides, Air Training Cadet Corps, accordion and fiddle club, sports centre, New Horizons Art Group, squash, tennis, hockey, rugby, football, golf, camera club, country dance society, a wonderful motocross track and club on the Longformacus Road, all the emergency services, a hospital and a health centre. There is too, a centre at nearby Putton Mill which includes a fitness centre, massage therapy, a golf driving range, group fitness classes and and sports' massage and last but not least, a children's play area and café known as Hurly Burly. The overall list goes on and on and I am so sorry if I have missed any out. For further details, best contact the wonderful town website at duns.bordernet.co.uk, another fine site in the Borders. That website compliments the site and work of the Dunse History Society who have contributed so much and have built a very impressive archive of a very impressive locale. The town also boasts one of the oldest Masonic Lodges in the country in the shape of Lodge Dunse No 23 who celebrated their 260th anniversary in 2011, a remarkable achievement indeed and still going strong.

*O*n top of the sports and other clubs, societies and amenities in the town, there are the three churches, which also leads to more social occasions. Then there is the impressive Public Park arguably the town's greatest asset and one of the loveliest in the Scottish Borders. The lands for the park, as we have seen, were purchased by Andrew Smith of Whitchester, a most philanthropic man as was Sir William Miller of Manderston who bore the cost of reclaiming the land from the marshes and then proceeded to fund the building of the main entrance gates and pillars with

Duns Bowling Club at the Public Park

~ *Today's Town* ~

the arms of the Burgh, Millers of Manderston and John Smyth. The lovely park, to the south of the town centre, is a large, well laid out place of recreation for all. It contains extensive grassland, a large kiddies' play park, tennis courts, formal gardens, the burgh's bowling club and three beautiful monuments as we have seen, all bearing a great deal of importance including the War Memorials, and the Fransciscan Order's tribute to John Duns Scotus, one of the truly great Scots and philosophers of all time. There are many benches situated all around providing rest and relaxation in the midst of beauty. The colourful Summer flower arrangements, well cared for hedgerows, a great variety of shrubbery and an amazing array of trees including Beech, Holly, Horse Chestnut, Larch and Yew. The park is overlooked by Boston Court which, in part, occupies the site of the Boston Church and proudly boasts the Drumclog Bell, **(right)** the bell of the old church which, once again, gives the town more connection with the Covenanters and their famous victory at the Battle of Drumclog on 1st June, 1679.

Many entrances are afforded the park, from all sides, including from the town centre at South Street and so many happy hours can be spent in the peace and quiet, A walk in the park is a gentle distraction from the bustle of every day life and perhaps, meeting new friends, as this humble man did; don't forget to take to the 'board walk', an extended walk from the park to Clockmill passing behind the new school in the process. The recreational and sporting activities of the old place is quite overwhelming, from the sports facilities, the wonderful Castle Wildlife Reserve, the peace and relaxation of the park all providing the key to fruitfulness and contentment. In Duns, the door to peace and happiness is never locked. Another 'sport' which is played in the town is the *Ba' Game* which had been enacted every year for centuries before its renewal in the 20th century.

Details of the great, the fierce, the awesome but funny game are page 57, contributed by the Dunse History Society Website.

Above : an old etching of original High School

Below : The first public library

Both courtesy of
Ronald Morrison and the Dunse History Society

~ *Annual Events – The Ba' Game* ~

With the days lengthening in times past, the inhabitants of the town would have been looking forward to, with anticipation or perhaps apprehension, to what was known as Fastern E'een and particularly perhaps to the Ba' Game which, by tradition, was always played on that date.
The date of Fastern E'een could always be calculated by the following rhyme :

> *First comes Candlemas,*
> *Syne the now mune,*
> *To the first Tuesday after,*
> *Is Fastern E'een.*

The following is an account taken from R.J. Johnston's Book, *Duns Dings A'*

"*Fastern E'een's Ba' Game was for centuries, prior to 1886, played annually in the streets of the town. It certainly existed in 1686 when a riot ensued after some alleged ill treatment of a man called John Bayne on 17th February, the date of that year's festival. Bayne was apparently dissatisfied with the disposal of his complaint by both the Baillie and the Sheriff and carried his case to the Privy Council, who dismissed it also.*
In 1886, a snowstorm prevented the Ba' being played on the due date. Probably the opportunity was taken to stop the festival as, apparently it had been falling in to some disrepute on account of a certain amount of drunkenness being associated with it.
The procedure connected with the Festival commenced about a week before 'the day' Three young men called the 'Ba Men' were chosen by the townsmen to make the preliminary arrangements. They met on the previous Wednesday to hold, along with their supporters, 'the shaping of the ba' when they all paraded around the town accompanied by a drummer and a fiddler playing,

> *'Never let the gree gang doon*
> *For the gude o' the toon'*

Thereafter, the Ba' men prepared the balls. Only three were required for the play but four were prepared. Of the three balls used, the first played was the gilt and called the 'Golden Ball', the second, from its colour, 'Silver Ball' and the third was spotted. The fourth was presented to the Superior of the town, or a member of his family, his Baron-Baillie if available, who threw the first ball.
The opposing parties were the married and single men. The goal for the former was the Parish Church which was left open for the purpose and one of the mills in the Parish for the single men. Those reaching the mill with a ball, were dusted by the miller as proof of their success (The others of course, had to get in to the church for their success) The prizes were, for the Kirking or

~ *The Ba' Game and the Summer Festival or Reivers Week* ~

The Ba' Game in action

the Milling of the first ball was 1/6d, for the second 1/- and for the third, 6d. The first ba' was thrown up a 1 o'clock. Prior to that hour, the shops had the shutters put over their windows and, in the absence of shutters, temporary boards were affixed to avoid breakage of their windows and other damage as the game was played with great vigour. In the evening, celebrations were held. These are described in a poem by R. M. Calder, the Polwarth Poet.

> An' then the ba' men wi thir friens
> adjourn to some, ane o' the inns
> Where Lang Syne yarns the landlord spins
> O' what he's done and seen
> An' when the noise and din has ceased
> Then pork and dumplings crown the feast
> Washed doon wi' toddy o' the best
> And a grand day was had by all

~ *Summer Festival (or Reivers Week)* ~

The Ba' Game seemed to disappear from the town's calendar some time in the 19th century but it was resurrected during the the early years of the 20th century when the 'Infirmary Festival' was inaugurated to raise funds for the local hospital and other medical establishments. That festival was enacted every year except the wars years but was finally ended in 1948 at the oncoming of the National Health Service. However, annual celebrations did not come to an end, the new Summer Festival, or Reivers Festival was introduced and has gone on unabated ever since on the first week of July. Earlier in the year, a young man and a young lady are chosen to be the Duns Reiver and his Lass, and, for the younger children, the Wynsome Mayde is selected. It truly is one of the great festivals of southern Scotland and never

~ Reiver's Week ~

fails to attract visitors from all parts joining the local people as they celebrate their town, their heritage and their proud history. The Duns Reiver is the greatest honour any young man or woman from Duns can ever be accorded and Duns was indeed, the first town to have a lady as the Reiver when Vikki Rybouska was installed in 1996. In 2015 Darren Aitchison was Reiver and his Lass, Stacey Wilson while the Wynsome Mayde was Mariah Rong and her Maydes of Honour were, Ailsa Dewar, Sophie Scott, Abbi Lindsay and Jenni Gray.

The festival, now known as Reiver's Week commences on the first Sunday in July with the traditional Kirkin' o' the Reiver, at the Parish Church, accompanied by his or her Lass or Lad, supporters and the Wynsome Mayde and her courtiers. Following the church service, the party then walks in procession amidst the cheering throng as the opening ceremony gets underway in Market Square. The highlight of the proceedings is the processional march of the Duns Pipe Band leading the town's dignitaries, holding aloft with great pride, the historic Burgh Standard. The Festival President then calls on the Duns Reiver to accept the Standard, to promise to keep it safe and to accept the responsibilities of his office as the town's ambassador for the next year, which the Reiver dutifully agrees. The Colours are then waved in salute to the cheering Dingers, Reiver's Week is underway, let the celebrations commence. Later that day it is time for the great family fun day when there is something for everyone to enjoy and compete, from toddler to senior citizens, this is one of the busiest, noisiest and happiest events of the week. The evening brings the first 'rideout' of the week, the family cycle run, again young and old together sometimes on the same bike. When everyone is home safe and sound, cheers ring out as the first day is coming to and end but there is another happy intrusion, a play featuring the Duns Players is held in the busy Volunteer Hall.

The Duns Reiver and his Lass passing the Sally Lodge

Monday brings the ladies and kids competitions at the golf club while the Kirk Café is open in the parish church hall. Between 10am and 2.00pm, a free play for the kids is held at Hurly Burly, a children friendly soft play area at nearby Putton Mill. In the afternoon, the Reiver and his entourage visit Knoll Hospital and Station Court, a supported living centre. The Knoll Hospital which caters for in patients, patients in need of some longer term care and a GP

~ Reiver's Week ~

unit, there is also a nurse led day clinic. When the principals have completed their visit to the sick and elderly they return to the town to accompany the Wynsome Mayde and her entire court to the public park for her crowning ceremony. Her court consists of crown bearer, sword carrier, courtier, pages, maids and flower girls. The Mayde will then join the Reiver in laying wreaths at the town's War Memorial in keeping with tradition. That area of the park where stands the memorial, is always busy with well wishers and sight seers and of course, mums and dads. It really is a solemn moment for the principals and gathered townspeople, as they remember their heroes who died on foreign shores. Then follows the judging of the best turned out pony and rider for the kids up to 12 years old, before the mounted cavalcade rides round the town led by the Pipe Band. The final event of the day, the Bed Race, organised by the ex-Reivers' Association, begins at 7.30pm outside the Barniken House Hotel building much to the amusement of the competitors and the spectators. This is usually the funniest of all events during the festival, so colourful, so amusing and, sometimes so bizarre. It's said the best things are left to last but in this case, best? certainly the craziest.

Everyone definitely joins the party on Tuesday, if not every other day, when there really is something for everyone. The golf club hosts the men's golf competition while the Kirk Café is open in the church hall. The Volunteer Hall, the principal hall in the town, hosts the annual Teddy Bears picnic for mothers and toddlers and where great fun is had with the kiddies hanging on grimly to their very own teddy bears while mum is busy setting out the picnic. Meantime, the Reiver, his Lass and their attendants are busy visiting the elderly residents at Lanark Lodge before carrying on with their tour of visitation. Music is always provided at a chosen venue, as the senior citizens while away their day dancing the light fandango...and perhaps, the Military Two-Step. As evening falls, Duns Football Club host their annual 5-a-side football competition, including the kids' fun football meaning everyone will not see, arguably the most historic event of all the entire festival, the rideout to Duns Law and the site of the original town, Bruntons. At 6.00pm prompt, the Reiver and his Lass with all their

Reiver and Lass at top of Duns Law
Courtesy of Ronald Morrison

~ Reiver's Week ~

supporters and followers, many of whom having travelled from other towns, ride up Castle Street. Once at the top of Law, at the Covenanting Stone, a service is held by one of the local clergy as a silent audience bear witness.

A courtesy bus is provided but many of the townsfolk have made the climb on foot to see the proceedings and pay homage to the events of 1639, when the heroes, under General Leslie, of the Scottish people and church, stood tall and were prepared to die in an effort to defy Charles I and his attempts to force his Canon Law on the people of the country of his birth. The principals then visit Bruntons where a solemn oration is made before the return to the town where a Gymkhana is already underway at

Ceremony on Duns Law
courtesy of Dunse History Society

Mainsgate Park but that is not the final event of the day, that honour goes to a family ceilidh in the Volunteer Hall. The whole family can attend what is another of the more popular events for all, where the hoochs and yeochs shake the hall to the rafters as happy people take to the floor to jig and reel to the rhythms of the ceilidh band. A great time is had by all but soon it is time to trudge home, arm in arm and full of cheer.

The following morning, Wednesday, sees the Wynsome Mayde and her court visit Knoll Hospital while the Reiver's entourage visit Mount View. Later that day, the parish church is the place to be if you enjoy strawberry teas or, if you prefer, there is the afternoon disco in the Volunteer Hall but don't forget to don your fancy dress. Like every other town, the fancy dress never fails to put a smile on everyone's face and you can be sure of some hilarious sights. Wednesday evening brings the time honoured Riding the Town's Bounds but before that, at 5.30pm, the judging takes place for the best turned out horse and adult rider with the David Lamb Memorial Trophy going to the winner. During the rideout, the Reiver, in keeping with tradition, cuts a sod at Harelaw Crags before the party visit Duns Castle to convey the respect the townspeople hold for the Hay family of Duns and Drumelzier. The Laird, in turn, reciprocates his family's greetings to the town. The return trip is made via the Bluidy (Bloody Burn) where the incident with the Earl of Northumberland's troops took place in 1377, and where some died causing the burn to run red for three days. On his return to town, the Reiver hands over the sod of turf for safe keeping. Time now for all the principals, Reiver's party and the Queen's court to visit Gavinton to pay their respect to the people of the lovely little village

~ Reiver's Week ~

where they are made most welcome at the village hall with the music provided by Duns Pipe Band. Meanwhile, Duns Rugby Club and Duns Football Club lock horns at the public park with the winners carrying off the The Thorburn Challenge Cup. Everyone knows footballers are more clever and sharper than rugby players but who will prevail on the night? What game will they play, will it be rugby football or football rugby, if you want to find out, get yourself along to the park, if nothing else, laughs and pranks are always high on the agenda. Following the match, the teams, and any other interested parties are invited to a quiz night in the, where else? Volunteer Hall. Wednesday has passed and another page has been written in the town's history, what will Thursday bring?

*T*hursday's activities begin a little later but nearly everyone who can, pops in to the many cafés, inns and restaurants in the town to discuss the week so far. For some, it really is a tiring week with so much to see and do. The Wynsome Mayde's Teddy Bear Activities begin in the public park at 1.00pm when all the children are invited to come along and have fun. Many races and special events are laid on with one of the more popular being the obstacle race. The next important rideout sets out from Market Square at 4.00pm when the Reiver and his Lass lead their supporters, visitors and anyone else who can come along, to Longformacus, the ancient village 'ower the hills' to the north. A friendly welcome is always given at the atmospheric wee place and the locals even lay on a barbecue, fingers crossed for good weather. Longformacus is still the sleepy wee village it has always been though now lacking its old village inn which was always a welcome sight for those who had just crossed the haunting Lammermuirs from Haddington, a route a priest took at least once a week for years as we shall learn in later pages. Travellers were always welcomed with warm open arms just as the travellers with the Reiver would receive, some things never change. Back at the town, the adults five kilometre race gets underway at 7.00pm, leaving from Hugo's café and wine bar in the Square, up Castle Road, past Clouds and into the castle estate. They then make their way round Hen Poo before passing the Glade and the return trip to Hugo's. That run follows in the footsteps of the junior fun run who have already made their way to the Pavilion entrance at the castle before returning to town.

*D*uns Pipe Band was founded before the First World War and one of their first Pipe-Majors was Tommy Campbell a veteran of the Seaforth Highlanders. The band have been going strong ever since and are a popular choice for many occasions. Tonight, Thursday, the band put on a performance at 8.00pm for their adoring audience, I am sure throughout that night and many others, the Dingers will surely remind everyone of their name, through their wonderful rendition of *Duns Dings A'*. The people I have conversed with in Duns are

~ *Reiver's Week* ~

extremely proud of their pipe band, one of the oldest in the Borders. At 10.30pm, one of the most popular of events gets underway, the Torchlight Procession through the town to the park where a bonfire and fireworks display awaits. Very few, if any, would miss this event unless something much more pressing came along. The wonderful spectacle is always well attended and, though it is late, the children have the time of their young lives, full of life and carefree, no school in the morning, though they can't stay in bed too long in the morning, they have another important date at 11.00am.

Friday morning arrives and first on the agenda is a free swimming lesson for all the kids hosted by the Wynsome Mayde, the hour long session is a very popular occasion for everyone concerned not least the Mayde herself. There is a break thereafter before a further re-enactment of the ancient and historic *Hand Ba'* in the Market Square and, as we have already seen, causes no end of excitement for all concerned.

At 6.30pm the single handed bowling championship gets underway at the bowling club when the old Town Council Cup is the prize for the winner so you can always be assured of a keen and hotly contested tournament. 7.30pm is the time for the big social evening of the week, the Reiver's Ball a formal occasion in celebration of the Reiver, his Lass and their supporters, a way of congratulating them on a job well done. The evening ends almost as a 'nicht afore the morn' occasion and more than one toast will be offered. The staff and cleaners must be 'worn out' after a busy and demanding week of events. That must be the case for all concerned though and the next morning does not offer a sleep in, the last day is a big day, and a very important one at that.

9.00am on Saturday is the starting time for the procession to Whitchester. All assembled, the mounted brigade and others follow the pipe band, in procession up Castle Street, Teindhillgreen, the castle estates, on to Cockburn Law where an ancient fort once stood, eventually reaching Whitchester House, once home of the philanthropic Andrew Smith and his wife Ada. In 1878, Andrew, an Edinburgh brewer, bought Whitchester and life, for everyone in the area, changed forever, for the better. Over the years, the new Laird of Whitchester financed great changes, not only for Longformacus Church but also funded the building of the village hall, a new kirk at Cranshaws as well as funding Whitchester Cottage Hospital in Duns and providing the money, as we have seen, to purchase land for the public park in Duns. He later made funds available to move the town's Mercat Cross in to the park. Such a wonderfully generous man, long will his name be remembered with great affection in the southern foothills of the Lammermuirs. A rideout to his former home near Ellemford, now a Teen Challenge rehabilitation centre, is a way of paying tribute to a great and so generous gentleman. On the return journey, the Community Council of Abbey St. Bathans, Cranshaws and Longformacus present the party with rosettes at the end of Cockburn Road. They get back in

~ Reiver's Week ~

time for the 6.00pm start of the Carnival Parade, full of colourful vehicles and folk, full of joy, full of everything that is good in the Burgh of Duns. The joyful procession is cheered all the way round the town by an excited throng of onlookers. This is just the beginning of the end; soon it is time for the closing ceremony when the Duns Reiver returns the Burgh's Standard, cheers ring around the Square, now it is time to party, from 9.00pm the Market Square is 'full to the rafters' as the music rings out and the happy folk just want to dance the night away. All good things do come to an end though and on the stroke of 12 midnight, the party music stops and the people stand with heads held high as they rejoice in the 23rd Psalm. Another year of a great party has come and gone; since 1949, the Summer Festival or Reivers' Week, has been growing stronger and getting better every year since it took over from the defunct Infirmary Week, itself of more than 60 years standing. Like every other town in the Borders, the end marks the beginning – now it is tine to begin planning foe next year's festival.

Sometimes, especially when there is inclement weather, festival events are held in Southfield Community Centre and what an inspiring place that can be. The house was built for James Robson, a local solicitor, in 1868 but only ten years later, when he died, the house passed to his son. He, James, handed the house over for convalescing soldiers during the First World War but soon after, it was sold to Frances Hay of Duns Castle who then passed it over to Berwickshire Education Department to house girls from outlying areas throughout the parish who attended the High School and stayed in the house during the week but returned home at the weekends. After many other uses, the magnificent 19th century mansion-house was converted to the town's community centre in 1977 and in that role, it remains. There are of course more clubs and associations in the town, as we have seen but two of them do attract visitors from near and far, like the Horticultural Society one of the oldest in the country, founded in 1842 and hosts their own show every September. Competition is fierce among the entrants many of whom have traveled long distances to exhibit their own particular fare. Categories include, flowers, plants, vegetables, handicraft, drawings, paintings, floral art, baking, preserves and so on. The show always attracts so many entries and audiences who come to view and, hopefully buy. Those shows are particularly popular in the Borders and is well worth a visit.

Duns Amateur Operatic Society perform many musicals around the region but they have their flagship performance in April every year at the town's Volunteer Hall. Founded more than 50 years ago, the Society also stage a Christmas pantomime in the town annually. Duns also boasts the Royal Scottish Country Dance Society and they too perform all over the region and further afield providing even more entertainment for locals and visitors alike.

~ The Berwickshire County Show ~

*F*inally, another great attraction in the town as we know, and a magnet for hundreds of visitors from all over Scotland and the north of England, is the Berwickshire Agricultural Association's Duns Show, held in the grounds of Duns Castle in early August every year. The Association is charitable and exists for the advancement of agriculture, the general improvement of stock and further developing manufacturing and pastoral care throughout the industry.

I wonder if you have ever thought of the work of farming in general. All we see is enclosed fields either under cultivation with every crop imaginable, or under pasture providing the space for sheep and cattle to graze. We may even see pig farms where the means, and little houses, are provided for the care and shelter of the animals. Yet there is so much more to it than that. Before the Agricultural Revolution of the 18th century, farming was haphazard to say the least and everything seemed to be carried out on one great field but one of the advents of the revolution was, field enclosure allowing crop rotation which resulted in better crops and healthier animals. The enclosing led to more efficient farms, larger and better crops, more country tracks and roads allowing us all more access to the beauty of our countryside; hedging and forest shelter belts promoted the further development of our birds and other wildlife; it was a win win situation for everyone and Scottish farmers, in the ensuing period, have produced the finest meat and vegetables in the world, a reputation well deserved and jealousy guarded. In a sentence, the farming industry has recovered so much land from the wrath of nature, developed and saved it for now and forever, for all of us to admire and cherish. From my very limited knowledge of farms or the fields, what I do know is, every field on every farm has a story all of its own, to tell. It is interesting to note, the Agricultural Revolution in Scotland was inaugurated in the main by John Cockburn of Ormistion, a member of the family of the Cockburns of Langton, old Barons of Duns.

*T*he great show consists of a livestock show combined with a day full of entertainment for everyone, young and old. It makes no difference if you are a farmer, office worker, villager or town dweller, there is so much on offer to enjoy and savour in a convivial atmosphere where everyone is a friend, for the day at least. So many acquaintances have been made at events such as this, which have lasted a lifetime.

A typical Duns Show consists of : Horse events of which there are many, livestock parading and judging, poultry judging, a very popular dog show open to breeders and amateurs and a very interesting industrial section. Other events include, a show of vintage farm vehicles and classic cars, trade stands, 'quack commandos', terrier racing, obstacle racing and lots of fun for the children including a Puppet Show. There are so many choices of food and drink stalls but, of course, you may bring your own picnic to enjoy in beautiful

~ County Show – Notable People ~

surroundings.

The Berwickshire Show, founded in 1895 under the Berwickshire Agricultural Association is a registered charity and, since the beginning, has been a very much looked forward to event. Over the years, the show has gone from strength to strength but is always looking for new members to join. It is one of the oldest of its kind in Scotland and the event, one of the best, remains, in many people's eyes, the most colourful and enjoyable family day out in the entire county.

~ Notable People by birth or association ~

We have already mentioned Elias de Duns, John Duns Scotus, Jim Clark and the great minister Thomas Boston along with the many Royals who visited the town and Randolph of Moray, nephew of Robert the Bruce and builder of the first 'modern' castle is be mentioned too, but here are a few more.

The original Barons, the Homes of Ayton must lead the way of notables in the more 'modern age' while the Cockburns of old, many of whom were born in the parish, were very important to the development of the town and district and, as we have seen, the development of the agriculture system. They owned castles at Langton and on what became Cockburn Law and were, for a time, Barons of Duns. They spread across south east Scotland and built other castles at Clerkington and Ormiston in Haddingtonshire. So many of the Hay family have, more than most, contributed so much to the town's development. The notable Hays are directly descended from the Hay family of Locherworth (Borthwick) through the Yester branch of the family. They have gained much acclaim over the centuries, across Scotland but more particularly in the counties of the modern Scottish Borders and East Lothian The present Chief of the Yester branch of the family, including the Hays of Duns and Drumelzier, is Charles David Montagu Hay, 14th Marquis of Tweeddale.

All the covenanting soldiers and their leader, Alexander Leslie, later Earl of Leven and Lord Balgonie must be considered truly notable. They were soldiers of *Christ's Crown and Covenant* and saved Scotland's National church. The Miller family of Manderston were very supportive and many good things in the town are the residue of their generosity. The benevolent Chrysties of Grueldykes also did much for the town as did Lady Grizel Baillie, daughter of Sir Patrick Home of Polwarth, who, with her husband began work on the building of Mellerstain House; she was a songwriter and a much loved friend of the poor of Duns and district indeed many of the Homes of Polwarth were benevolent lords; I think it would be fair to say though, all the other aristocrats of the region, like the Homes of Wedderburn for instance would have much constructive input in the town's progress over the centuries.

~ *Notable People* ~

*O*ther notables included Abraham Robertson (1751-1826) mathematician and astronomer, Thomas McCrie the elder, great minister, historian and writer of the lives of John Knox and Andrew Melville, he was born in 1772 and died in 1835; Rev. Ralph Erskine, another of the great ministers of his day also preached the gospel in the town, but not in the parish church, he was non conformist and joined the growing group who opposed the continuing patronage of the local aristocrats. Rev. James Gray (1770-1830) poet and linguist who was also master of Dumfries High School and Edinburgh High School was another notable who was a good friend and confidant of Robert Burns. Cadwalleder Colden who was born in Ireland while his Duns born parents were on a visit there, was Colonial Governor of New York for a time in the 18th century while James Grainger, a poet and linguist, was born in Duns in 1721 and became a prominent figure in English Literature. James Dickson, a general in the East India Company, and who bequeathed so much to Duns, was another. Many members of the very eminent family of Ainslie of Berrywell were born in the town giving so much over the years. They boasted in their midst, doctors, lawyers and James, one of Australia's first labour immigration agents. More well known Dingers include John Black (1783-1855) journalist, John Brown (1735-1788) physician, Samuel Cockburn (1823-1919) doctor and homeopath, Robert Hogg and Robert Fortune both 19th century botanists, Sir John Pirie who became Lord Mayor of London in 1842 while others excelled in the sporting field. Those include Andrew Cowan, rally driver, Louise Aitken-Walker, racing driver, and business lady in the town, who has the distinction of being the world's greatest lady driver; and yet another racing driver, Euan Thorburn. Cecil Dixon a well known cricketer and two professional footballers, Tom Lockie and John Wightman all added to a very impressive list of Dingers. Robert Burns also visited the town but we shall hear more of the Immortal Bard, probably the most famous of all Scots and who is the subject of much education all over the world, at the Parish Church.

*A*s we have now seen, Duns, though small, is a more than impressive community, and has been since the beginning. It has produced a string of notable people which is testament to a fine education system since early times. The mix of blood over the centuries, particularly the early comings and goings, as we witnessed earlier, has served the town's population well over the years right up to the present day and will continue to do so in the years which lie ahead. Unlike its predecessors, the modern town of Duns will never die; its past and present will always be treated with the greatest respect by everyone concerned in the town, Duns is in indeed, in good hands.

*M*any of the notables of the town we have seen, would be baptised in the old kirk and it is to that church, the Parish Church, we now head.

~ *Today's Churches - The Parish Church of Duns* ~

*I*n times long ago, all the more humble parishioners would gather round tiny, busy Church Square on Sunday mornings awaiting the arrival of the local lairds, who would make their way to their very own lofts, embellished with their respective coats of arms. The lairds would be followed in to church by local dignitaries, local businessmen then, finally, the poorer classes. The reason I make the point is, the church at Duns was one of the very few churches where the poor were always allowed inside to worship when the lairds were about, and they even had their own pews, democracy personified..

*O*ne Sunday, in the Spring of 1787, another notable man associated to the town, Robert Burns, attended the church with his friend, Robert Ainslie and Robert's family including his father, Robert snr., his mother and sister Rachel. During the service, the minister, Rev. Robert Bowmaker was scathing in his attack on the congregation and Duns folk in general, citing a less than perfect lifestyle amongst many. Young Rachel appeared to take the attack personally when Burns saw her, agitated, nervously turning the pages of her bible; the sight of the young lady caused Burns to utter :

> *"Fair maid ye needna tak the hint,*
> *nor idle texts pursue,*
> *'Twas guilty sinners that he meant.*
> *not angels such as you"*

Later that day, a still thoughtful Burns uttered an attack of his own on the minister when he said "A man of strong lungs and pretty judicious remark; but ill skilled in propriety, and altogether unconscious of his want for it" So typical a remark from such a thoughtful man. It is widely believed, Robert Burns penned the poem *To a Louse* was based on that incident at Duns Kirk.

*R*obert Bowmaker was the minister who heavily criticised the populace in general when writing in the Statistical Account of Scotland in the 1790s. He cited drunkenness, poverty and idleness and blaming the 27 ale houses in the town as the root cause. He may have had a good point but he appeared to aim his wrath at everyone, Burns however did make his own point, as always.

*W*hile the Parish Church has been mentioned in earlier pages, it must also be said, the church, as so many others in Scotland, was the first home to the Parish School which was originally, situated on the site of the church hall and was almost certainly the oldest known school in the town. That arrangement would arrive some time after the Reformation of 1560 when free education for all was being rolled out in every parish across the whole of Scotland though there is a thought there was some education offered during the Catholic years in the shape of a medieval school which is said to have stood in the same compound as the present church. It is not quite clear when the original church was built but we do have knowledge of much renewal and renovation over the

~ *Today's Churches* ~

centuries including the Burgess Loft which was added in 1593. Fragments of the old church still remain in the churchyard particularly the Wedderburn Burial Aisle just a few yards to the south though a patron of the kirk during the 19th century, one, David Milne Home, begged to differ suggestions that the Home Burial Aisle was ever part of the old kirk. As a matter of note, other notable families in the graveyard are the Hays of Duns and Drumelzier and the Millers of Manderston. There are so many other very old gravestones in the peaceful kirkyard including tables, symbolic, urn and obelisk forming a place of serenity near the town centre.

Duns Parish Church from the south

A new church, the present, was built in the late 18th century to replace a late medieval church and was almost certainly the third church in Duns but was almost wholly destroyed by fire in 1879, only the outer walls and tower remained, but was completely restored the following year; an inscription above the south door confirms the dates of building, destruction and restoration.

At first I found the exterior of the church something of an extravaganza and it was difficult to know exactly what shape it was with so many apparent 'add ons'. Even from an aerial photograph, it is difficult so I can best describe it as, essentially a rectangle with a transept added on the centre of the building to the north and a large section added to the south where the tower abuts from the main building and is sided by two round head, mullioned windows with two higher, double round head, lancet type windows, one to the east, the other to the west. Around the other three elevations, the church and other buildings including the church halls, are extremely well lit with so many windows, most of which are groups of two tall round heads, all square-leaded with more

~ *Churches* ~

elevated lights serving the lofts. The main entrance to the church is from Church Square at the west of the building. The hall to the east, as we have already discussed, is on the site of the old school perhaps even the same building. The church itself has three entries, one to the west, as mentioned, and the others on the north and south elevations.

*O*n entering the church, there is no doubting the shape of the building, it is in the form of a 'T' with the beautifully carved pulpit dominating the south wall flanked by two magnificent round head windows with 'Y' mullion and centred at the top by a round cinquefoil window, all containing the most stunning stained glass. There are two communion tables, one from the old South Church, both with matching chairs. An octagonal stone font sits proud to the west of the communion area while a lectern stands opposite with another brass lectern sited on the Communion Table. Below the wester most section of the south facing windows is a lovely Celtic Cross dedicated to Rev. Hugh Mackay who died in 1999 only a year after retiring as minister at Duns having served the parish for 30 years. There is an organ, the first in a Scottish Church when it was installed in 1867, and grand piano on either side of the communion area joined, interestingly enough, by a full drum kit and a screen where video productions can be shown. The real eyecatcher on that wall though, is the most unique ensemble of organ pipes I have ever had the privilege of witnessing. They look almost like fine porcelain with the most elaborate mosaics all around lending some extra colour to the body of the kirk.

*T*here is a large gallery mounted around the east, west and north sections, providing nearly 500 extra seats though that area is seldom used these days. On the subject of seats, or pews... On 14th October, 1610, some of the seating within the kirk became a point of contention between the Cockburn family and the Home family of Wedderburn. A huge argument broke out during the minister's sermon when, with swords drawn, the families caused an unholy uproar. They were later called before the Privy Council when the Home brothers were fined 5,000 merks each and ordered to keep the King's peace and not to interfere or molest the Cockburns while Sir William Cockburn was ordered to provide security of 3,000 merks to ensure his three sons kept the King's peace and did not interfere in the lives of the Homes. Only weeks earlier, the two families played against each other at a game of *'the futeball'* which ended in drawn swords. It can be safely said, the Homes and Cockburns were not bosom brothers. Some years later, in 1683, the Cockburns were at it again with another pew dispute with one, William Ancrum, but that still was not the last of church disputes, that dubious honour went to George Trotter and George Swine after Trotter, an elder during the Episcopacy, was caught fighting, in 1692, with elders of the now Presbyterian church.

*T*he Queen's and Regimental Colours of the King's Own Scottish Borderers, which were presented to the regiment in Berlin in 1975, now adorn the church

~ *Churches* ~

as does the Burgh Standard. The colours were presented to the KOSB by HRH Princess Alice, Duchess of Gloucester who was the regiment's Colonel-in Chief. Another wonderful connection with the regiment, which was amalgamated with the Royal Scots in 2005, is the unique stained glass windows, joining so many other wonderful stained lights, erected in the memory of Lt-Col. Peter B. Gow, King's Own Scottish Borderers, by his widow Mrs. Olive Gow. The windows were created, not as whole plate glass but by dozens of small pieces welded together, which represent the regiment's history, their place in the infantry brigade of the British Army, the Rose of Minden and, in fact everything including the band around their bonnets. That incredibly wonderful work of art was created by Douglas Hogg of Gordon. The windows were unveiled in the same month in 2005, as the amalgamation with the Royal Scots, it is almost as if a Divine hand had guided the time of the unveiling and unification to coincide thus making this the last memorial to the KOSB as an independent regiment.

Colonel Dow was a long standing parishioner and elder of Duns Parish Church. As a final act of togetherness, the KOSB regimental association provided and fitted bullet proof glass on the exterior of the building to protect the windows, thus carrying out their time honoured duty, of guarding and protecting.

The church roof is high and, unusually, there is an extremely large roof light giving out a warming glow in a very bright church. The roof is of plaster and beam with large corner section units which may have held candle lights in days gone by. The walls are embellished with plaques in memory of parishioners, ministers and to the war dead of the parish while a glass unit displays the church's treasures, community plate, jugs and cups. To the north-east of the building are two halls, a session room, vestry and the old Beadle's apartment, which is still used as a private home

Hay family of Duns Castle Burial Ground at Kirkyard

The old church commands a view to the south overlooking the old junction of Murray Street, Bridgend and Station Road, a scene which lasted for some centuries and viewed by so many ministers and parishioners, but has now been closed off to form a much needed car park.

~ *Churches – Parish Church - Christ Church* ~

We read earlier of how Collegiate Churches and their Prebendaries, including Duns, appeared to have some leeway in the wake of the Reformation. In the case of Duns, the immediate post Reformation preachers were known as parsons or vicars and the first man known as minister was Rev. John Bennet but he lasted less than a year before the former minister at Edrom, Patrick Gaittis took over and served the local parish until 1611.

The present minister, the latest in a long line, is the Reverend Stephen Blakey who also takes services at Edrom and Bonkyl Kirks both of which are united with Duns.

~ *Christ Church* ~

Christ Church is a member church of the Scottish Episcopal Church and is situated on Teindhillgreen to the north-east of the town centre. It was founded as a Mission in 1852 meeting in a hall roughly on the site of the future church. In 1857, William Hay of Duns Castle instigated not only the building of the church but also the design based on a church he had seen and sketched on the River Rhine in Germany. The result of his vision is a quite stunning church sitting proud above the road to Preston. The

Christ Church from the south east

magnificent, 5-bayed, south elevation is flanked to the east by a smaller, set back 3-bayed chancel and, to the west, a large, two stage, square tower with squat cone shaped spire and weathervane finial on top. The first, lower stage, contains the wonderful Norman style arched entry while there are louvred windows above on the south and west elevations. A lower window, on the west, lights the stairway to a former choir gallery at the west side of the nave, which is now used as a meeting room. The feature windows of the church are the most beautiful rose window on the west gable below a stone cross finial and the great three light pointed window with the most elaborate carvings on the east gable, again topped by a stone cross finial. It really must be emphasised however, Christ Church is indeed blessed,with some of the most beautiful stained glass windows in Berwickshire.

~ *Christ Church - Our Lady Immaculate & St. Margaret* ~

. The building is high roofed above the central passage while lower sloping roofs on the north and south cover the east facing pews in the north and south

The pews are separated by the central aisle which is flanked by two rows of cream sandstone pillars holding arches forming a most elegant scene.

The most atmospheric Chancel, entered by one step under a great arch, is highlighted by the magnificent stained glass windows and overlooked by a half barrel, painted ceiling. The stained glass to the north and south elevation do enlighten proceedings beautifully, though some say they dim the light making the church rather dark. There is a fine octagonal pulpit on the north and a brass lectern to the south with a lovely, carved marble font situated at the west end of the nave which contains many wall memorials to local families, like the Baillies, Baillie-Hamiltons of Mellerstain and the Millers of Manderston for instance; there is also a tribute to the war dead of the parish.

Chancel at Christ Church

Like the parish church, Christ Church, one of 300 Anglican Congregations in Scotland, has a lovely, respectful burial ground to east, west and south containing many beautiful and interesting stones and family burial grounds forming a most peaceful setting even though it overlooks a principal route. The congregation can be very proud of their wonderful church.

While the first known vicar was Augustus E. Crowder who served the congregation from 1852 until 1874, the present Priest-in-Charge at Christ Church, which is part of the Worldwide Anglican Communion, is Rev. Dr. Kenneth G. Webb

~ *Our Lady Immaculate and St. Margaret Church* ~

The town also benefits from the lovely little red sandstone Roman Catholic Church at Bridgend, Our Lady Immaculate and St. Margaret. When building began on the the church, it was planned, at a future date, to enlarge the structure to the south since it was envisaged it would become a much larger congregation and what we see now was intended to be the nave with an archway which lead to a south chapel. As it happened the archway in time was

~ Churches ~

blocked by unforseen circumstances.

Though looking small from the outside, it is a rather spacious interior, bright and a most welcoming place of worship where the congregation were originally formed of Irish immigrants and a priest from St. Mary's Church in Haddington rode across the Lammermuirs at least once a week for several

Our Lady Immaculate and St. Margaret, Roman Catholic Church

years to serve the congregation. When the church was built in 1882, It was intended, as we have seen, to ultimately be enlarged and a beautiful Gothic type arch was created as the entrance to a new south chapel which was never erected. The reason behind that area never being utilised was the fact, immigration from Ireland virtually 'dried up'. Nevertheless, it really is a lovely church, with lovely feeling of peace as if a greater force was 'on guard'

To the east of the chapel stands a wonderful reredos which was once a marble fire place in the sadly lamented Langton House. It is embellished with a Holy Crucifix and forms a striking altarpiece behind the altar, a truly beautiful piece of work. Also within the church, is a stained glass window referring to John Duns Scotus' passionate defence of Our Lady's Immaculate Conception, statues of Our Lord, the Virgin Mary, Joseph and Child and St. Margaret of Scotland. The congregation is fiercely proud and supportive of their church and why not? they are embraced on all sides, in the arms of goodness. The first listed priest I could find, was James MacDonald who served to parish for two years from 1917; the present priest, Father Robert, is much respected, and a warm host who sincerely bids a very warm welcome to one and all.

~ *Churches* ~

The first sight I had of the church, did not take my breath away but inside is a different matter. It does exude a comforting warmth after stepping from the top of windy Bridgend and the feeling of well being is quite overwhelming. A few minutes within the hallowed walls are priceless in terms of feeling welcome and wanted. All around, the symbols of peace look down over the holy house and contentment does indeed reign. Like the other churches, the congregation are so at home in their beautiful church, a very special part of a very special 'Holy Trinity' in the old county town.

Marble Reredos

at

**Our Lady Immaculate
and
St. Margaret Church**

~ *Great Houses - Duns Castle* ~

*I*t is most suitable to begin this section with the town's very own castle, one of the great houses of Scotland which has been inhabited for nearly 700 years and, while we have already seen some of the following, it is most important to relate to the castle in its own right.

*T*he beautiful Castle of Duns is amongst the most stunning of its kind in the entire country with most of the works being carried out by the Hay family, adding to and enhancing the original L shaped tower keep. Many believe, like MacGibbon and Ross, in their book, *Domestic and Castellated Architecture of Scotland,* that the tower on the east end is the original which was built between 1316 and 1320, though with more modern facings designed to blend in with the rest of the building. Others though, and the Royal Commission appears to concur, that tower is of the 16th century. My own opinion, if I may, is, the main fabric of the tower appears original but with much refurbishment as MacGibbon and Ross

**The East Tower
with much of the original fabric**

suggest. Those works of the 14th century were carried out by Randolph of Moray and his wife, Isabel. The castle was in the hands of the English during their so called campaign of the *Burnt Candlemas* of 1356 but was not thought to suffer damage though much work was carried out after Hertford's dastardly attack in 1545. That incident was described in a document of his 'achievements' of 1545 when it is noted *"and Monday, Downes towre and towne, awaretrowne (overthrown) and birned when ither touns and villaiges were birned. Next day wys West Nysbet and East Nysbet which were birned......"* That in itself meant there were works needed to bring the tower back up to scratch but that does not mean it was rebuilt at that point. The Home family would carry out works and the Cockburns of Langton may have carried more works during their tenure but virtually everything we now see is the works of the Hay of Duns and Drumelzier family who have improved the building several times throughout the centuries always maintaining the ancient tower to the east. The biggest undertaking, which formed what we now see was undertaken between 1812 and 1818 when the eminent architect, James Gillespie Graham was engaged. He employed local builders and craftsmen to

~ *Great Houses* ~

undertake the building works, including builder, William Waddell, John Steel who created the internal wood carvings and John Anderson who carved the most sublime gargoyles. No doubt, some time after completion, Laird William Hay, a notable sketch and paint artist, would add his own hand to the building adding some extra colour to the interior. William as we know, was the man who was responsible for the design of Christ Church.

Today, the castle and estate play host to, not only wildlife enthusiasts and walkers, but also, as we have seen, the Berwickshire Show. It is also one of the country's top venues for conferences, parties and weddings, and a very popular and romantic venue it is with some of the most wonderful walks to be had in one of most gently scenic estates in the country.

Of course, there is more to the estate than 'merely' the castle, and there are several other buildings of note including the entry lodges, but the courtyard,

A section of the Screen Wall entrance leading to the Courtyard

Period house in a corner of the beautiful Courtyard

the former stabling and service area, now with several dwellings, is a simply beautifully constructed building complete with spire and bell tower with the courtyard entered by a Gothic arch. There are too, seven self catering cottages including the aforementioned Pavilion Lodge, St. Mary's House, the Coach House, the White House, Azelea and Cedar Cottages and the atmospheric Carriage Mews. I must add, the great curtain wall stretching to the west of the main entrance and which contains the entrance to the walkway to the Stables Courtyard, is another magnificent construction, probably the most architecturally supreme wall I have ever had the privilege of witnessing. It is an eleven bay crenelated screen with buttresses separating each bay. Half way between house and the west tower, there is a squared tower like gateway

~Great Houses - Duns Castle - Nisbet House ~

leading to the stables topped by an exquisitely designed pillared lantern type tower.

In a few words, the Castle of Duns is wrapped in the warmth and beauty of a truly magnificent estate, the majesty of which is rarely equalled.

The following history articles for a selection of other great houses in the immediate area and their occupants, are given with the kind permission of Dunse History Society. The Society's words are shown in italics.

~ Nisbet House ~

The Nisbet (or Nesbett) family can trace its history back to the time of Gospatrick, Earl of Northumbria in the middle of the 11th century. In 1139, King David I of Scotland granted a charter in favour of Aiden de Nisbet of the lands of Nisbet on the north bank of the River Blackadder. The Nisbets seem to have built two castles, one at East Nisbet (now Allanbank) now vanished and one on the site of the present house at Nisbet (formerly West Nisbet) Initially the property would comprise only the mediæval Peel Tower but this was substantially altered in the 1630s by Sir Alexander Nisbet of that Ilk who added a fine new fortified mansion incorporating the peel. Sir Alexander was a strong supporter of King Charles I but suffered heavily for his support of that ill fated monarch, his son, Sir Phillip Nisbet being executed at Glasgow after being taken at the Battle of Philliphaugh. Captain Robert Nisbet, being captured with Montrose and executed at Edinburgh and Major Alexander Nisbet being killed at the Seige of York in 1644. Sir Alexander was forced to sell the property in 1652 to John Ker. In 1774, a classical square tower of the style of William Adam was added to the west end. The house remained in the Ker (or Carr) family until 1950 when the estate was sold to Lady Brockett and, after some modernisation resold in the 1960s. The property is still in private hands.

Nisbet House - Courtesy of Becky Williamson

~ *Great Houses* ~

*I*t is interesting to note that in 1784, the main block of the house, some three kilometres south of Duns, was built on the site of an old castle which was surrounded by a moat. Local architect, Thomas White then designed a bridge for Miss Carr to cross a local burn, the Howe Burn and a lake created with the water being drawn from the burn. The lake and formal garden were situated over the site of an old canal which had been filled in.

*T*hree members of the family, Jone, William and Thomas, all desginated *de Nesbyt* swore fealty to the 'Hammer' if 1296.

*A*lso mentioned earlier, two battles took place at Nisbet, both known as the Battle of Nesbit Moor, the first taking place in 1355 and the second in 1402. The first Battle of Nesbit Moor emanated from a dispute between the powers of England and Scotland over the release of David II who had been captured by the English at the Battle of Neville's Cross in 1346. negotiations between the countries broke down early in 1355 which prompted the English to attack, burn and destroy much property in the own of Patrick V, Earl of March. The earl quickly assembled an army ably assisted by William, Lord Douglas and Ramsay of Dalhousie and some fifty French knights. They stormed Norham Castle and destroyed the town before retreating and leading the English in to an ambush. The ensuing battle on Nesbit Moor became a rout and most of the English army were either killed or, the more senior, transported north to Edinburgh. The ordinary English yeomen were caught by the French and slaughtered on what became known as Slaughter Hill. Their reasoning was, one of their own French officers had been killed and butchered at Neville's Cross. Those battles at Neville's Cross and Nesbit Moor were a direct result of Scotland's *'Auld Alliance'* with France which made the English, who were at war with France, just a little nervous of a dangerous enemy knocking at their back door.

*T*he second Battle of Nesbit Moor arrived in 1402 and, in relative terms, was a fairly minor affair. The battle took place on the Slaughter Field on the Kimmergehame Estates as a form of retaliation following Scots' attacks in to the north of England at Northumbria and Cumbria. On return from one of those forays in Northumbria, the now forfeited lord, George de Dunbar, 10th Earl of March, led two hundred English knights based at Berwick, against a Scottish force of 400, mainly spear men with some knights on horseback. The English easily won the day but that caused a huge back lash from the Scots when they invaded the north of England. They caused so much damage but were ultimately stopped and defeated at the Battle of Humbleton Hill later in the same year.

*W*e witnessed the words of Hertford, about his works at Duns where he also claimed the destruction, in 1545, of the Castle of West and East Nisbet. While Nisbet was restored, the castle at Allan Bank was not though a large house was built in later times.

~ *Wedderburn Castle* ~

*Wedderburn House is a very fine Georgian mansion-house dating from 1771, designed by the renowned architects Robert and William Adam.
The Humes of Wedderburn can trace their line back to 1413 when Sir David Hume of Thurston in East Lothian, second son of Sir Thomas Hume of Hume, received a grant from Archibald, Earl of Douglas, of the Barony of Wedderburn, a grant which was confirmed by James I of Scotland in 1430.
At that time, the castle was a simple peel tower and a white stone plaque from that date can still be seen in the present courtyard and it is thought that the haha (ditch with a concealed wall to stop cattle and sheep) surrounding the castle and which may follow the line of the original castle palisade.
Sir David's grandson, also Sir David, who married Isabella Hoppringle of Smailholm in 1481, was the eldest of seven sons known as the 'Seven Spears of Wedderburn'*

Wedderburn Castle

The principal entrance

enshrouded below dark, dramatic clouds

All seven brothers would appear to have fought at the Battle of Flodden in 1513 when Sir David was killed as was his brother, Sir George. Reference is made by Sir Walter Scott to the Seven Spears in his heroic poem, 'Lay of the Last Minstrel'

> *"Vails not to fell what steeds did spurn
> Where the Seven Spears of Wedderburne
> Their men in battle-order set"*

In 1517, the family was very heavily implicated in the murder of Chevalier de la Bastie, effectively, at that point, Governor of Scotland. His head remained in Hume Castle until 1810 when disposed of by Mrs Jean Hume.

~ *Great Houses* ~

Those were indeed troubled and difficult times – during the years, from 1413 to 1576, every first born son was either killed in battle against or a prisoner of the English. However, it was also also a period of expansion for the family viz their acquisition by forced marriages of the estates of Blackadder and, slightly earlier, Marchmont.

The 10th Baron, Sir George Home, declared for the Jacobite cause of the 1715 uprising but was captured at the Battle of Preston, tried for treason and his estates made forfeit. However, for once being in debt proved to be a lifeline. His estates at that point were bonded to his cousin, the Rev. Ninian Home of Billie and it was decreed in those circumstances, the Crown could not foreclose and George was also granted a pardon.

Work on the present building commenced in 1771 by the 13th Baron, Patrick son of the above Ninian although much the greater part of the building was overseen by Patrick's nephew, George, while Patrick indulged himself in Grand Tour of Europe acquiring in the process many great works of art including perhaps in particular, the chimney pieces.

The great building was known as Wedderburn House until the early 19th century when it was renamed Wedderburn Castle with reference to an older building which once stood on the site. The works on the present building of Adams design was overseen by James Nisbet, the site superintendent, who also supervised the building of another old domain of the Home family, Paxton House.

Motto above main entrance
'Remember, True to the end'

Wedderburn is a magnificent example of an Adam castellated building with round towers on each corner and a larger, square tower at the main entrance reached by an impressive, arched portico. Another entrance, leads through an archway in to the courtyard of what is essentially a 'U' shaped building with one elevation simply a wall, effectively designed to appear as a 'roomed and windowed' section of the house. The building deceptively hides the courtyard where once the old castle stood. The whole estate contains architecture of the highest quality including the stable block and the entrances with the wonderful Lion Gate to the north a real eye catcher. Wedderburn Barns is a sublime venue

~ *Great Houses* ~

and can be hired for all occasions including weddings and corporate hospitality as indeed can the big house. The Barns enjoys the company of lovely cottages where the most peaceful holidays can be spent. Adding to that is the wonderful estate lands containing a vast array of plants and trees and the remnants of an unusually large walled garden still containing some fruit trees and a very large section of the original wall.

The great house is still in the own of the family after all those centuries, in the shape of David Home Miller, son of the previous owner, Georgina Home Robertson, and his wife Cat Macdonald-Home.

Relaxing Courtyard at Wedderburn Barns

Having experienced Wedderburn in a small way, I can say the welcome is gracious, warm and very genuine

Magnificent arched entrance to the Quadrangle at the great house

Interestingly the eminent Homes are not the first family to reside on the lands of Wedderburn, another clan lived there from as early as the 11th century

~ Great Houses ~ Wedderburn ~ Kimmerghame House ~

and known simply as 'de Wedderburn'. Reference is made to them in August, 1296 when Walter de Wedderburn swore fealty to the dreaded 'Hammer', Edward I of England. Other references to the family arrived in 1364 in the name of John of Wedderburn then of William of Wedderburn in 1426 around the time the family left their Berwickshire lands forever, moving to Angus where in time, a branch of the family were elevated to the Earldom of Dundee.

~ Kimmergehame House ~

The house with most of its contents including many valuable works of art and furnishings, was largely destroyed by fire in 1938 as a consequence of a workman's error during the installation of electricity.

The lands and estate of Kimmergehame came into the ownership of the family of Swinton in 1776 when Archibald Swinton of Manderston married Henrietta Campbell of Blythewood in Glasgow. The Swintons are an ancient family who can trace their roots back to Eadulf I, King of Northumbria in the year 896AD and are the Swintons who were so named for their achievement of clearing the area of wild boar. The creature is prominently in their coat of arms with the motto j'espere – je pense.

Henry de Swinton was one of the thirteen names put forward in 1291 for the arbitration of Edward I of England as to rightful Guardian of Scotland following the death of Margaret, so called 'the Maid of Norway' and he swore fealty to Edward. Later however, the family supported Robert the Bruce during the Wars of Independence. Sir John Swinton, 14th of that ilk, fought for John of Gaunt, distinguishing himself at the Battle of Noyon and was a commander at the Battle of Otterburn in 1388 but gallantly fell at Homildon Hill in 1402.

Sir John, 15th of Swinton, fought against the English at the Battle of Bauge in 1421 and reportedly slew the Duke of Clarence, brother of Henry V of England. The event is recorded by Sir Walter Scott in his poem 'The Lay of the last Minstrel'

> *'And Swinton laid the lance in rest,*
> *That armed of yore the sparkling crest,*
> *of Clarence's Plantagenet.*

He was however, killed three years later at the Battle of Verneuil where the Earl of Douglas also fell.

During the time of the Civil War, the Swintons initially supported the Royalist cause and Sir John, the 19th of that ilk fought and was taken prisoner at the battle of Worcester in 1651. He later however switched allegiance and is recorded as being 'one of Cromwell's most trusted men' but come the Restoration, his estates were made forfeit and he was incarcerated in

~ *Great Houses* ~

Edinburgh Castle for six years. His trial and imprisonment feature in Scott's novel 'Heart of Midlothian'

The estates were restored however following the Glorious Revolution of 1688 and Sir John 25th of that ilk, was one of the founders of the Bank of Scotland in 1695.

During the course of the French Revolution, Captain George Swinton, at great risk to himself, helped many to escape the guillotine and the book, 'The Scarlet Pimpernel' is believed to have been largely inspired by his heroics.

In more recent times, perhaps one of the more distinguished members of the family, unfortunately now not nearly as well remembered nor recognised as he should be, was Alan Archibald Campbell-Swinton (1863-1930) who as early as 1908, described an electronic method of producing television. He, rather than James Logie Baird, has, at least some claim to be regarded as the true inventor of television.

Kimmergehame House
© Harry Swinton – Wikipedia

When Kimmerghame House was largely destroyed by fire in 1938, the nearby Stichill House was in the process of being demolished and stone from that house was used in the partial rebuilding. Equally, just over a year later, during World War II, as Charterhall Airfield was being built a few miles away, stone from the unrestored part of Kimmerghame was used in the construction The house remains in the own of the family.

From, at least the 17th century, Kimmerghame was a domain of the Home family (it is known to have been the home of Sir Andrew Home in 1730)

There is a fine mill steading, adjacent to the main entrance to the estate, which was largely built in the 19th century and contains the most atmospheric tower. To the south of the mill, there stood Kimmergehame Chapel and burial ground. The chapel, built in the early 12th century, was granted to Herbert de Camera in the earlier part of the 13th century by the monks of Durham Cathedral. Two centuries later, the St. Clairs of Herdmanston in East Lothian, were granted the right, by the Diocese of St. Andrews, to raise a Templar tenament and the gift of lands at Kimmergehame.

~ *Great Houses - Kimmergehame - Manderston House* ~

It was to that family, the St. Clairs, to whom the tiny Kimmergehame estate hamlet was named, Sinclair's Hill. **(left)** The tiny settlement, which still exists, included a school. Latterly a hall and two rows of very fine houses but look out for the one topped off by a large white stork. There is also an ancient well and a house with the pride of the hamlet's title emblazoned on the front wall. It really is a pleasant wee place, full of peace, full of grace. It is situated to the south of Kimmerghame Mill and is well worthy of a look. The old houses blending well with newer homes to the west do tend to add that little more security for a long term future.

Another interesting note of the great house and its owner, arrived in 1997 when thieves secured entry to the house while the family were asleep. They made the silly error of entering the bedroom of the man of the house, one Major General, Sir John Swinton, the Lord Lieutenant of Berwickshire. They awoke him from his slumber and, in his own words recalled the moment, "I woke from my sleep to find intruders in the room, I reacted pretty strongly with a yell and they scarpered" How dare they intrude on one of Scotland's oldest, if not the oldest, family. The noble family of Swinton, who are descendants of Cospatric of Northumbria, who was in turn, ancestor of the Homes, 'came home' in the wave of a long and complicated curve, when they purchased Kimmergehame House and estate from their 'distant cousins'

Sir John Swinton and his wife, Lady Judith, are the parents of award winning actress, Tilda Swinton. We shall learn more of the great family in the village of Swinton pages.

~ *Manderston House* ~

Manderston House has been described as the 'final flowering of the country house' being built between 1903 and 1906 on a budget of 'no expense to be spared'. The architect was John Kinross.
The lands and estate of Manderston were originally held by the Hume family and it is recorded that Janet, daughter of Sir John Home, married, in 1622, Lord Renton who was later proposed as Lord Chancellor of Scotland, a

~ *Great Houses* ~

proposal however, blocked by the Earl of Lauderdale on the grounds, Renton 'had not the fortune to bear the rank'
By the mid 18th century, the property would have been a simple peel or tower and appears as such in General Roy's map of 1750. The property, for a short time, passed in to the hands of the Swinton family of Kimmerghame and around 1790, a substantial dwelling house was built for Dalhousie Watherston to the design of either Alexander Gilkie or John White.
In 1855, the estate was purchased by Mr. Richard Miller, merchant, son of James Miller of Wick and Elizabeth Sutherland, daughter of Rev. William Sutherland, minister in Wick. On Richard's death, Manderston passed to his brother, William Miller. William Miller had made a fortune trading in herring and hemp particularly with Russia and was subsequently appointed British Consul at St Petersburg. Sir William was a considerable collector and there are a number of items which he brought back from Russia still on display in the house including, in the entranceway, a pair of a child's sledging seats. On his return from Russia, he became M.P. for Leith and, latterly, for Berwickshire. In 1874 he was created a Baronet by the Prime Minister, William Gladstone for political services rendered although it is reported that at no time, did he ever make a speech in the House of Commons.
In 1871, Sir William added a pillared entrance porch, a new French Renaissance style roof and additional servants' accommodation to the design of the architect, James Simpson.

Manderston House -From a 1911 postcard – Dunse History Society

On Sir William's death in 1887, the estate and title passed to his second son, James Miller, his eldest son, William having died by choking on a cherry stone while still a schoolboy at Eton. Sir James was described in Vanity Fair in 1890 as 'A good fellow, one of the most wealthy commoners in the country and a bachelor. He is a very eligible young man' He also had the epithet, 'Lucky Jim'

~ *Great Houses* ~

Sir James had married Evelyn Curzon daughter of the 4th Baron Scarsdale and sought to provide for her a home, the equal of the family house, Keddleston Hall in Derbyshire.

Sir James swept away the alterations of James Simpson and instructed John Kinross to design the present house using a design excellence and best craftsmanship on a lavish scale made possible by an open budget and 'no limit in cost' There 400 workmen were employed at the height of construction and the total cost worked out at £221,000, three times the original estimate. Before instructing John Kinross on the building of the house, he had asked him 'to prove his worth' by designing a stable block which was subsequently described 'as perhaps the finest stable block in the world' The house itself was built to the very highest standards of the time incorporating many innovations including electricity, central heating, running water and modern conveniences.

The most striking features are perhaps, the silver staircase, the only such staircase in the world, the luxurious and sumptuous state rooms, the magnificent ballroom and the exceptionally fine kitchens.

E*very section of this great house was unsurpassed for quality of material and workmanship. It set new standards in building technique and ingenuity, which others have strived to match but rarely equalled. The house was completed in 1905 and 7th November, Sir James and Lady Miller hosted a great ball to mark the event. Unfortunately, two months later, Sir James was to die of a chill caught when out hunting at the age of 42. Sir James and Lady Miller had no issue and on their deaths, the house passed Sir James' brother, John Alexander Miller who subsequently died in 1918 again with no issue and the estate in turn passed to his sister Amy Elizabeth Miller who was married to Thomas Manbourg Bailie from whom the estates descended to the present owner, Adrian Palmer, the 4th Baronet Palmer. The house contains the largest collection of Huntley & Palmer biscuit tins in the world and also the world's largest collection of Blue John Ware. Blue John, or bleujaune, named after its colour, is a semi precious stone found only in Derbyshire. The collection was put together by Lady Evelyn Miller, building on the collection which already existed at her family home at Kedleston.*

Cottage by the lake
Courtesy of J. Thomas. Geograph

~ *Great Houses* ~

The house has been used as a set in several films and featured in the acclaimed Television series 'The Edwardian Country House' when a number of actors lived for several months in conditions recreated as far as possible, as they would have been in Edwardian times and which gave a most interesting insight as to what life both upstairs and downstairs would have been like at the time.
The house is open for public viewing in the summer months.

There is more to Manderston than the house of course, including the beautiful gardens, atmospheric lake and water features, wonderful cottages and farm buildings and an estate par excellence providing excellent walks in the midst of some wonderful old trees. The gateway to the walled garden, as all the other gateways to the estate, is just another precious stone in the Manderston crown. Add all that to Buxley House and all its associated buildings, farm and cottages and, would you believe? a cricket club complete with pitch and pavilion. Perhaps the most noted feature buildings on the estates, quite apart from the principal dwelling places, are the Marble Tower and Dairy, the great quadrangle of the stable block neither of which will go unnoticed on a tour of one of the finest estates in the country.

The Marble Dairy and Tower
The tower is well over one hundred years old and was built so the lady of Manderston House could entertain female guests after dinner, free to chat without being overheard by servants!
The Marble Dairy is in the basement of the tower, cool air rises from it, keeping the room above, at a low, even temperature all year round; in the days of tightly laced corsets and many layers of clothing, the coolness kept the ladies more comfortable and less risk of fainting. The tower was reached by a stroll through the formal gardens or, if the weather was wet, via a firm surfaced path around the cricket pitch and up the steps guarded by two unicorns - Photo and words, courtesy of Barbara Carr, Geograph

Manderston, apart from opening to visitors in the summer months, is also available for hire for any function be it corporate or private use as a dinner or for wedding celebration.

~ *Great Houses – Blackadder House* ~

Blackadder House was a magnificent classical Palladian house which stood on the estate of Blackadder approximately one mile south of the village of Allanton.

The name was no doubt taken from the nearby water of the same name which etymologically is an interesting combination of the English word 'black' and Brythonic or Welsh word 'aweder' meaning water perhaps indicative of an overlap between the two peoples. The Blackadder's sister river, the Whiteadder running out of the Lammermuirs is so called as tumbling off the hills. It is white and frothy in appearance whereas the Blackadder meandering its lugubrious way through the rich farmlands of the Merse, runs slow and dark.

The name Blackadder has perhaps acquired a degree of levity thanks to the antics of a certain Rowan Atkinson and the much acclaimed television comedy series of the same name. The history of the family however is almost every bit as unfortunate in its own way as anything whichever befell Blackadder or Baldric. Rowan Atkinson, on being asked why he chose the name for the series replied that he was looking for a name reflecting 'a rather Errol Flynnish character'

The earliest record of the name can be traced back to 1225 and the grant of the present lands of Blackadder in 1452 by James II of Scotland in favour of Cuthbert Blackadder the so called "Chieftan of the South"

An old plate of Blackadder House – courtesy of Dunse History Society

In 1513, Andrew Blackadder fell on Flodden Field leaving a widow and two young daughters. The Humes, whose part at the Battle of Flodden has been questioned, saw their opportunity, attacked and killed the immediate heirs,

~ *Great Houses* ~

assaulted the castle and imposed forced marriages on the widow and the children. Sir David Home of Wedderburn marrying the widow and his two brothers marrying the daughters albeit they were both only eight years of age. The Blackadder family continued to maintain their ownership of the estate including petitioning Parliament but after various murders, assassinations and cunning plans eventually relinquished it and, in 1671, Sir John Home was created Baronet of Blackadder.

The castle remained in the possession of the Homes over the following centuries until being acquired in 1836 by the Houston, later Houston-Boswell family.

Until around the mid eighteenth century, the house was probably little more than the original peel and plans were drawn up for the complete remodelling by James Playfair but never effected.

The old Summer House and section of garden terraces

courtesy of James T.M. Towill, Geograph

The remodelling was however, subsequently carried out in accordance with plans drawn up by Robert Adam and extended by John Lessels in 1853 and it was he who ballastraded the terraces and added a large asymmetrical wing. The house which was described as 'The Stately Home' was probably the first in Berwickshire to have electric power and the original power house survives. The house was requisitioned during the First World War for the accommodation of troops and considerable damage was inflicted. No compensation would appear to have been forthcoming and the house was demolished in 1925. Today, all that remains are the estate cottages, a stable range with tower and and obelisk steeple attributed to Alexander Boswell in 1785, a walled garden and summer house.

Robert Fortune, the famous horticulturist, was born on the estate in 1812 but the cottage in which he was born, has disappeared.

*A*mong other members of the Blackadder Clan who were assassinated to prevent any challenge to the Home 'takeover' at Blackadder, were Robert and

~ *Great Houses* ~

Patrick, respectively the Prior of Coldingham and Dean of Dunblane Cathedral and both sons of Robert Blackadder, 1st Archbishop of Glasgow. They, like Rev. John Blackadder who convened the great conventicle at East Nisbet, were all members of the Tulliallan branch of the great family.

**Left:
Blackadder House, 'looking out'
Courtesy of James T.M. Towill**

Below Left:

Magnificent Twin Lodges at South Lodge Blackadder

While the old 'town' of Blackadder and its chapel, which was subordinate to Edrom Church, has gone, several of the Estate Farms still exist including, Blackadder West, Blackadder Mains, Blackadder Bank and Blackadder Mount all containing beautiful farm houses and cottages and of course the clock tower at the Mount's stable block. They are joined in the present day by some atmospheric lodge houses and some of the most interesting ruins anywhere including the power house, garden terraces and a gracious summer house though there are no signs of the old town nor chapel.

91

~ *Great Houses - Langton House* ~

The earliest, recorded owner of the lands of Langton was one Roger de Ow in the reign of King David I of Scotland. In turn they passed to the family of Vipont (De Veteriponte) who held them until 1314 when Sir William Vipont, Lord of Langton, was killed at the Battle of Bannockburn. Through marriage, they passed in to the hands of the family of Cockburn.

During a dispute in 1517, when the castle was being besieged by one branch of the family against another, the French knight, de la Bastie, acting on behalf of the Regent Albany, sought to intervene but in the ensuing events was, as we have seen, murdered by the Homes.

In November of 1566, on her return from Jedburgh to Edinburgh on her journey through the Eastern Borders, Mary, Queen of Scots spent a night at Langton. One report states she was accompanied 1,000 horsemen but this number seems excessive.

The first Langton House was probably built at the beginning of the 17th century and Hearth Tax records of the time show the house as having 23 hearths making it the second largest in Berwickshire.

In 1745, the 7th Baronet of Langton was killed at the Battle of Fontenoy fighting for the forces of the Duke of Cumberland, the victor at Culloden the following year. Following the Baronet's death, the estate was put on the market and purchased by one David Gavin who had made his money through trade. He immediately set about demolishing and rebuilding Langton House. He later married a daughter of the Earl of Lauderdale and their daughter married the Earl of Breadalbane.

In 1888, a subsequent Earl of Breadalbane set about building a completely new house to the designs of the renowned architect, David Bryce R.S.A.

Langton House – Dunse History Society

~ *Great Houses* ~

In Articles of Roup of 1924, a copy of which is in the Society Archives, the house is described as:
'Built of stone and slated roof with mullioned windows and ornamental stone terminals to the gables and stone chimneys in the style of the 17th century with more modern additions to the rear containing hall, picture gallery, four reception rooms, billiards room, boudoir, gunroom, ten principle bedrooms, six single bedrooms, five dressing rooms, 13 servants' bedrooms, four bathrooms, nine wcs, five housemaids' pantries and ample domestic offices'
The Policies and pleasure gardens are well laid out and include numerous lawns and walks as well as an en-tout-cas tennis court. There is also an excellent walled garden extending to about four acres divided by Yew tree hedges. There is a range of glasshouses conveniently heated and arranged for fruit and flowers and there is also a potting shed etc.
Outbuildings comprise estate office, gas man's cottage, garage for three cars with loft over, tool house, boiler house, harness room and men's rooms Two loose boxes and two stalled stables and two, five stalled stables.
Other buildings included another boiler house, food store, byre for twelve, byre for eight, workshop, estate sawmill, piggery, log shed, gas works, cart shed, tool houses etc.'
In 1876, a Wellingtonia or Giant Redwood, was planted by the, then Prime Minister, William Ewart Gladstone, on a visit to the property. This is on the left hand side of what was the main driveway and still survives. In 1990, it was recorded as 119 feet in height.

Principal entrance to Langton Estate and Gladstone's great Wellingtonia

The great house was demolished in 1950.

~ *Great Houses - Marchmont House* ~

The present Marchmont House was built by the third Earl of Marchmont in 1750. The second Earl had originally commissioned the renowned Scottish architect William Adam to draw up plans but the costs had proved excessive and the Earl died before any work had commenced. It is now believed that the building was designed not by Adam but by Thomas Gibson but whether or not, the house very much reflects Adam's influence. Of particular interest in the house is the decorative plasterwork by Thomas Clayton particularly perhaps the saloon which is decorated with family heraldry and military trophies while above are monograms of the 3rd Earl and his wife.

Prior to the commissioning of the building the present grand house, the family and their predecessors had lived in nearby Redbraes Castle., now ruinous.

The earliest recorded family at Redbraes were simply styled 'of Polwarth' Later passing in to the hands of the St. Clairs through marriage around the end of the 14th century. In the early years of the following century, the estate fell in to the hands of two very marriable heiresses. Their uncle, not wishing to see the estate pass out of the family, imprisoned them in his own castle at Herdmanston near Haddington. Nonetheless their hands were sought by David Hume of Wedderburn and his brother Patrick with whom the heiresses obviously were previously acquainted and on whom they would seem to have looked favourably. The two Hume brothers arrived with a band of followers and forcibly released the two heiressess returning with them to Redbraes where they were married. Nearly one hundred years later, as seen, the Humes were to acquire the estates of Blackadder through the forced marriage to the heiress. The Marchmont Humes were strongly of the reformed faith and in 1675, the second baronet, Sir Patrick found himself imprisoned in the tolbooth in Edinburgh for his activities in opposing the vicious suppression of the Covenanters by the Duke of Lauderdale. In 1683 he was suspected of involvement in the Rye House Conspiracy, an alleged plot by leading Whigs to prevent the succession to the throne of the future James II or VII who had openly converted to Catholicism. His life being very much in danger, Sir Patrick put out that he had gone on a long journey whereas in reality, he had

Redbraes, Courtesy of Becky Williamson

~ *Great Houses* ~

*immure in the crypt in the nearby Polwarth Church, a situation known only to his wife, his daughter, Grizel and his servant, Jamie Winter.
In this vault he languished for several weeks, food being smuggled to him at great danger to herself and the family, by his daughter Grisel before he managed to make an escape to London, Paris and then to Holland.
In 1688, at the time of the Glorious Revolution, he returned with William of Orange. William obviously had high regard for Sir Patrick, not only immediately restoring him him to his estates which had been made forfeit but, in 1677 appointing him Lord High Chancellor and Earl of Marchmont. He also showed his gratitude by allowing him to display an orange bearing the Imperial Crown on his coat of arms. The coat of arms can still be seen on the gable of Polwarth Church.
Sir Patrick took a leading role in bringing about the the Union of the Parliaments in 1707 before dying in 1724 at the age of 83. He was succeeded by his third son, Alexander who, in turn, was succeeded by his son, Hugh, the third, and last Earl of Marchmont and it was he, Hugh, who built the present Marchmont House.*

Marchmont House, as it is today

Sir Hugh was very much involved in politics being the Member of Parliament for Berwick and was one of the opposition leaders, in the House of Commons, to Sir Robert Walpole. He was also a close friend to the poet Pope and was spoken highly of by Dr. Samuel Johnson. Sir Hugh was married twice and by each marriage, produced one son. His son by his first marriage predeceased him and there was a bitter family quarrel involving his son by his second marriage so much so, Sir Hugh disinherited and named as his heir, his sister, Lady Anne who had married Sir William Purves of Purves Hall who later assumed the name Hume-Campbell, Later to be Hume-Purves-Campbell and

~ *Great Houses* ~

finally, Sir John the 6th and last of the Baronets, adopted the name Home-Purves-Hume-Campbell, before he died in 1960.
Further alterations were carried out by the architect, William Burn, the pioneer of the Scottish Baronial style of architecture between 1834 and 1842.
In 1913, the property was sold to Robert Finnie McEwan who instructed further changes to the design of Robert Lorimer who, among other alterations, added a top floor and and converted the stable wing to a double storey music room.
During the Second World War, , the house was requisitioned for use by John Watson's School, Edinburgh. The pupils may have been recognised some of the architectural features as their school in Edinburgh was one of the works of the same architect, William Burn. In the 1980s, the house was sold to the Sue Ryder Foundation for use as a nursing home. The property was closed as a nursing home in 2008 and has now been aquired by the owners of Marchmont Estates.
Currently the house and gardens are said to be, being restored to former glories. The house is surrounding by the most beautiful landscape and what was especially fine gardens. The Green Ride, the road from Greenlaw, passes along great avenues of trees while the Marchmont Avenue is a mile long walk through two great lines of magnificent, mature trees. The Doo'cot is a sight to behold as is the pond to the north of the house and the old Marchmont Railway Station a little south which closed in the 1960s but still the station house and platform survive. The station is now a private residence.

Above :
Marchmont
Doo'cot –
Courtesy of
Walter Baxter
Right : Old
Marchmont
Railway Station
with house and
section of
platform

~ *Photographs of present day Duns* ~

Tolbooth House on the junction of the Square and South Street

The former Dunlop Trust Hotel In South Street

~ *Photographs* ~

Above : The Working Men's Institute in the Square
Below : The Volunteer Hall

~ *The Villages* ~

~ *Abbey St. Bathans* ~

Situated some seven miles north of Duns, the tiny hamlet, enclosed in the hills, lies unhindered by the hustle and bustle of the modern day. If ever a place was locked in heavenly peace, it is the blissful community of Abbey St. Bathans. Perhaps that is why Baithéne mac Brénaind or Bathan, chose this wonderful spot of seclusion, to build his holy compound.

The wee 'church town' boasted one of the earliest, if not the earliest, Christian house in the Scottish Borders when Bathan, cousin of Columba, founded a small chapel in the late 6th century before becoming the 2nd abbot at Iona in 597AD. That foundation became the roots of a Christian community in the area which has withstood the tests of time and while the local church has sadly closed in recent times, a community still exists after some 1,400 years,

The tiny settlement in the hills is essentially a continuation of an earlier story; it is widely believed a community has existed here since the Neolithic period and many artefacts have been uncovered including a dagger up to 4,000 years old. In the 19th century, the remains of the 6th century chapel were found, the foundations measuring 18ft x 8ft with walls up to 5ft thick looking as lonely as the area in which they were laid, in what is the most cloistered part of the Berwickshire countryside. That find, just a few hundred yards south of the existing church, was on a site now known as the Chapel Field. It is not clear when the chapel was abandoned but it was 'lost' before Ada, wife of Patrick, 1st Earl of Dunbar 'stumbled' upon the holy place in the late 12th century. Believing of St. Bathan's presence, she was encouraged to establish a house of Cistercian nuns in 1184 during the reign of her father King William I (the Lion) Another house of nuns, including a hospital, existed at nearby Strafontaine which was governed from Dunglass, but that establishment closed no later than the 16th century. There was also a holy well near the site of Bathan's church near what became known as the Pilgrim's Path.

Over the years, Ada's enclave, which was a daughter house of Berwick, grew in importance, though never reaching the stature nor opulence of Berwick, Coldstream or Eccles, it was still deemed important enough to have a prioress of its own. Many of the prioresses were known as Ada, one of whom was called to Berwick in 1296 to kneel at the feet of Edward I of England and swear fealty to the dastardly king. She was joined on that occasion by Thomas of Bothans, a later master of Bothans. Over the years, so many more heads of the convent appeared to be known as Ada as if in honour of their gracious and pious founder.

Such was the importance of the holy cell, many charters gave us so much knowledge and a better understanding of the *Holy House in the Hills.* In 1214, in a charter of North Durham (Coldingham) a piece of land at Billie was gifted

~ *Abbey St. Bathans* ~

to the Priory while, a little later, of even more lands of Billie which were granted by Bothans, as the enclave was then known, to Durham Cathedral. Another special, though sad event, arrived in December 1214 when the founder's father, King William (the Lion) died. Weeks of prayers were conducted followed by hymns of celebration to the life of a man who ruled Scotland wisely for 49 years. In 1235, Johannes, Master of the Nuns, was ordered to pay for the teinds of Billie which had earlier been gifted to Coldingham and Durham.

*T*he priory was set in the most wonderful idyll, below the wooded hills on the banks of the Whiteadder and surrounded by rich arable land. Food was plentiful on both land and in river, more than enough to fulfil the needs of the sisters and the lay members of the community. Life was as serene as the days were fulfilling and soon more arrived to join the community in their work and live in the safety of a holy cell. Peaceful seclusion though, did have its pitfalls and many men travelled the route through the hills, hoping to avoid detection but when they reached the Priory of St. Mary, they demanded food, succour and shelter; of course their demands would be met by the ever forgiving sisters. Armies too, trudged that route and often threatened the security of the nuns. In 1333, in the days following the Battle of Halidon Hill, the nuns begged the protection of Edward III of England; the normally unforgiving king granted them their wish but not in perpetuity. Two hundred years later, the forces of Henry VIII arrived and devastated the ecclesiastical site at the start of the Wars of the 'Rough Wooing' when Henry demanded the Scots allow the infant Queen Mary marry his son Edward. The priory was never repaired, probably because religious upheaval was on the horizon and those present would have no appetite for rebuilding simply to leave for others.

*S*oon after the destruction, the lands were granted by Elizabeth Lamb, the prioress, to the Home family of Wedderburn who held them until the early 17th century before they, in turn, gifted them to Elizabeth Home and David Lindsay, son of the Episcopalian Archbishop of Glasgow. That couple, in the wake of the Reformation, styled themselves 'prior and prioress' of a secular community which no longer existed as a priory.

*I*n the meantime, the newly established church had taken

Kirk of Abbey St. Bathans

100

~ *Abbey St. Bathans* ~

over the priory chapel and rebuilt on part of what remained and used the renovated building for their new form of worship, the reformed church at Abbey St. Bathans was born! The first cleric at the kirk was William Colville in 1563 followed by Rev. Matthew Liddell in 1570.

During the time of religious renewal, the lands were constantly changing hands until finally in 1768, they passed in to the possession of the Turnbull family who built a fine house in the latter part of the 19th century. That house continued in the family through marriage to the Gillons well in to the 20th century but in the modern day, the house of Abbey St. Bathans has been subdivided in to four apartments though still, there is no hiding the beauty of a great building.

Abbey St. Bathans House

The church building itself is Romanesque, essentially a rectangular building of rubble whinstone, with a north chapel and a two stage, conical roofed tower added to the north-east with a porch and vestibule to the south-west. It was generally renewed in the early 17th century with more restoration work carried out in 1675 and 1699. It was completely renovated in 1719 and full glazing added a few years later when a bell too, was installed. During later renovation work, the stone effigy of a prioress was removed from a wall and placed in a specially made alcove in the east wall, which, originally, was the west wall of the old priory church. That effigy helps remind us of the history and origins of the foundation. The apexed roof is topped by grey slates and a cast finial on the west gable.

The old kirk is entered by a lovely porch leading to the vestibule where there is a stone, dedicated to the Rev. George Home who died in 1705. A central aisle splits two sections of pews facing east and a pointed archway near the north-east forming the entrance to the north chapel and vestry. The pulpit occupies the south-east corner near the centrally placed, finely carved communion table and octagonal timber font. The walls are white plastered with lower dado timber panelling under a magnificent timber, hammer beamed roof. The building, which was largely renewed in 1858 to a design by architect, John Lessels, contains some of the most wonderfully elaborate

~ Abbey St. Bathans ~

stained glass windows. The kirkyard contains many interesting stones and is the final resting place of the eminent Turnbulls of Abbey St. Bathans. Sadly, the Kirk has now closed after serving the people of the hamlet and surrounding farm communities for countless centuries though still serves the community when it is used to host various events and shows.

The wee fermtoun lies on the eastern stretches of the Southern Upland Way, the most important public walkway in the south of Scotland and is a magnet for hikers from all over Britain and beyond. A hostel once provided a place of rest and sustenance for the walkers but alas, has recently closed and is now a private residence. The lovely pedestrian suspension bridge nearby, helps walkers on their way across the Whiteadder Water.

The community forms part of the Preston, Bonkyl and Abbey St. Bathans Community Council while the church was part of the Kirk of Lammermuir with Cranshaws and Longformacus, linked to Polwarth and Langton;

Since the foundation of the priory, a small settlement grew and was probably not much larger than the community of today. Agriculture, livestock and arable, was always important as was logging and that has never changed with the farmers still working the lands while a local sawmill is kept busy.

Weavers too were industrious in the past but that is no more than a distant memory' Quarrying too was important in the old days as were the mills including one slightly to the north at Strafontaine near the old free kirk which now

The Old Schoolhouse with the old school behind
By kind permission of Mr and Mrs Dobie

exists as a private home. During the 19th century, when the hamlet was at is peak, facilities were a lot better than they are now when the two churches, were 'open for business'. a school too existed along with many mills all adding to a small grocers, a vitner who, it is believed, hosted a small inn, which some say, may have been situated at or near Moorhouse. There was also library, a

~ *Abbey St. Bathans – Allanton* ~

carrier and mail messenger to Duns and Grantshouse, and all the farming trades. Apart from what has already been mentioned of the present day, there is a village hall, a carpet bowls club, Boys Brigade and a branch of SWRI while an annual quiz is held in the hall while other activities of course, are walking and fishing. The Dobie family are the principal family in the present day and it is they, through farming and the sawmill, who provide the local employment. Interestingly, the old school stands on what was once the main route to Grantshouse.

Perhaps the most prominent person in the tiny place leaving aside Bathan, who went to be Abbot of Iona and Ada, daughter of a king, was David Hume or Home of Godscroft (1558-1629) who authored the *The History of the House of Douglas*. He was also a political theorist, poet and, for ten years, a Protestant pastor in France: Godscroft House still exists and the estate is home, in part, to a wonderful holiday haven at the Burnet Cottage. Nearby, Riverside Restaurant provides a warm welcome and excellent food while to south east is historic Retreat House, former hunting lodge of the Earl of Wemyss, which lies just north of the awesome 2nd century Edin's Broch Hall and the ancient workings at Cockburn Law nearby.

The rock laid by St. Bathan in the late 6th century has provided the foundation which has held firm in the shape of a stunning wee wee kirk building, standing proud in the seclusion of the hills but sadly, no longer providing the spiritual needs of the people in the small hamlet and surrounding parish.

The Retreat - ©2012 Jim Barton – Geograph

~ *Allanton and Allanbank with Broomdykes Farm* ~

The very mention of Allanton evokes thoughts of the now demolished Blackadder House, for which part of the village of Allanton was built. There is no doubt a community lived there from early times though the handsome village we now see, is almost exclusively from the mid 18th century and through the 19th. During the 19th century, the village contained all the necessities of its then modern life, including a blacksmith, two stone masons, a carpenter, cartwright, two millers, two weavers, dressmaker, three tailors'

~ *Allanton* ~

businesses, a beer house, a vintner, two grocers, a miller, baker, a doctor, school master and of course, a school, in fact there were two schools in the mid 19th century, one for girls only. There is even suggestion a small bank existed in the village at one point. There was also a Free Church of Scotland a little to the south of the village at the junction of the Broomdykes Road.

*T*he beer house was 'reborn' as the Red Lion Hotel with stable and a hay loft for the travellers' horses. As time passed a post office was introduced to what became known as the 'Tailor's Toun' before the Red Lion's stables were converted to a fire station. Add all that to the many nearby mills on the Blackadder and Whiteadder Waters and the many farms, meaning work was plentiful but virtually everything around was owned by the great Blackadder Estate, one of the largest such holdings in southern Scotland. There was even a small village known as Blackadder to the west of Allanton.

*T*oday, the schools survive, one as the village hall and the other, a private home, the church was converted to stables in 1954 though is now a dwelling place and the Red Lion has been reinvented as the Allanton Inn, the principal focal point for the local and surrounding community. The inn is managed by very enterprising proprietors and as recently as June, 2015, held a great *'Beer Festival'* which attracted many to sample 22 beers including many local ales and the excellent food which was on offer over the weekend. The owners hope that successful festival will be the first of many and become one the highlight annual events in the Duns and Chirnside vicinity of Berwickshire.

**Ladies assemble outside Allanton school on the right, now the Village Hall
Courtesy of Maggie Maan**

*T*he village comprises, essentially, a main street with a couple of small streets leading off including Blackadder Drive which is guarded at the entrance by two lodges for the old estate. The surprising delight of the main street is the differing architectural styles of the houses and cottages meaning a keen interest can be maintained for the inquisitive visitor. There is a fine varied selection with the new, matching well with the old, meaning there is an excellent

~Allanton – Allanbank~

blend throughout. Look out for the houses which still, proudly, carry the name of tailors' businesses, Allanton's principal claim to fame; in days long gone, people travelled from all over Scotland to be fitted for a suit from an Allanton tailor. Other delights in the village are two lovely wells but the one near the kiddies' play area at the south side is the one which catches the eye, so beautifully cast and enhanced with lovely flower arrangements. Incidentally, if ever visiting the lovely village, look out for the houses with the fishscale slated roofs, they are the ones which were part of the great Blackadder Estate.

Allanton is situated less than two miles south of Chirnside and is reached across the Allanton Bridge at the confluence of the Whiteadder and Blackadder Rivers but it is the bridge to the east, the Blackadder Bridge, we now take to reach the lovely little hamlet of Allanbank where the first building to catch the eye from the bridge is the beautiful Allanbank Mill House (now a private residence. **(below)**

*T*hat tiny community is a place full of surprises, full of wonder, full of history but, in the present day, could surely make claim to being the 'Arts Centre' of the Scottish Borders but more of that in a while.

The Well at Allanton
Courtesy of Maggie Maan

*A*llanbank or, to give the area its original name, East Nisbet, is situated on a neck of land locked between the two rivers, Whiteadder and Blackadder, and is one of the most historic of all settlements on the Merse. As we noted at Nisbet House, two battles were enacted on the lands between the two Nisbets with the lands of Kimmerghame 'hosting' much of the hostilities. In 1355, the larger of the two battles was principally engaged at East Nisbet where the Scots, under Patrick, Earl of March and William, Lord Douglas carried the day but in the second Battle of Nesbyt

Allanbank Mill
with Allanbank House in the background

105

~ Allanbank ~

(Nisbet) Muir in 1402, a much smaller affair, the Scots were vanquished by an 'English' force commanded by the traitorous George de Dunbar, 10th Earl of Dunbar and 4th of March. Many of the combatants, the Nesbyts, Dunbars, Humes and Swintons all participating in both battles, were lineally related, all descended from the same Northumbrian roots.

East Nisbet was indeed an important locale long before the battles and so many names have found their way in to the National Archives. Men such as Adam Nisbet, the son of Thomas, proprietor of Nisbet, was named in many charters of North Durham (Coldingham) from around 1235, then came John, Adam's son, who submitted to Edward I in 1296 along with Gilbert of East Nisbet. The earliest known mention of anyone in connection with East Nisbet however, was Arkil, the Grieve, who bore witness to the election of John as Abbot of Kelso in 1160AD.

The Nisbets built castles on both their estates of Nisbet and East Nisbet but, while the magnificent house at Nisbet still stands tall and proud, the castle of East Nisbet, which appeared on old maps as having been the larger of the two, has long since departed the scene. A chapel too, dedicated to St. Mary, was built on what is now known as Chapel Haugh at East Nisbet where the family of Nisbet and their estate workers worshipped for centuries. It was first mentioned in 1130 as a dependency of Edrom Kirk and was still in use beyond the Reformation but, in time, fell in to ruin, the site, on the banks of the Whiteadder, was finally cleared in the 19th century.

The Nisbet family fell from grace during the Bishop's Wars of the 17th century, when taking the side of the king and were essentially in agreement with the Episcopacy in Scotland. During those "Killing Times", they fought on whatever side were opposed to the Covenanters who were fighting to retain their own Presbyterian way of worship. Sir Phillip Nisbet was captured and executed in the aftermath of the Battle of Philiphaugh in 1645 while the head of the family, Sir Robert, was taken prisoner with James Graham, Marquess of Montrose and both were executed at the Old Mercat Cross in Edinburgh in 1650, after being found guilty of High Treason. As we have seen at Nisbet House, the end was nigh for the Nisbet (or Nesbyt) family and they soon sold that house to the Ker family though, it appears, the Blackadder Estate administered East Nisbet for some years before the Steuart family of Coltness bought the lands, now known as Allanbank, in, or around 1676.

Robert Steuart (or Stewart) 7th son of Sir James of Coltness was created 1st Baronet of Allanbank in 1687. His father, Sir James was, at that time, Lord Provost of Edinburgh and was held in the highest esteem throughout Scotland in the years before the Union of the Crowns in 1707. Robert himself entered politics and went on to represent North Berwick in the first Parliament of the United Kingdoms of England and Scotland.

Robert, who's family were directly descended from the early High Stewards

~ *Allanbank* ~

of Scotland meaning he was of royal stock, lived an interesting life which ultimately was bedevilled by a 'ghost' as we shall see. During his tenure he rebuilt the old castle in the style of the day and set about rebuilding some industry for his estate workers which resulted in some small time quarrying and mining for marl, neither of which was overly successful. Upgrading farming techniques in the area was attributed to the Stuart family while the nearby farm and hill of Stuartlaw was named in the family's honour. Three mills existed, a corn mill, a paper mill and a saw mill but they too have passed in to history though the mill lade still exists as does the large mill house alongside the old Allanbank Mill Steading. The lands passed on through the Steuart family until the death of the 5th Baronet, Sir John James, who died in 1849 though the great house was sold a little earlier.

*B*efore the Steuarts were entitled Baronets of Allanbank, one of the greatest of all Conventicles ever held, was conducted in the fields of East Nisbet but this Conventicle was rather out of the ordinary in as much, it was not planned as a Conventicle as such but as a Communion in the Fields. Nearly 4,000 people attended and literally hundreds of tables were set out with the wine and bread in readiness for great men of the cloth, Rev. John Blackadder of Tulliallan, acting in the shadow of his spiritual home, and two of the other great Covenanters, Rev. John Welch of Irongray who was a great grandson of John Knox, and Thomas Riddell who now lies buried in the Covenanters' graveyard at Greyfriars in Edinburgh. Those three brave men and thousands of communicants gathered in the fields of Allanbank in 1670 knowing the dreaded dragoons could appear at any time however they did take precautions. Long before the Communion Blanket Sermon was held, makeshift guard houses were erected to house covenanting soldiers with orders to keep an ever watchful eye on the comings and goings in the area. It is supposed, one such building which was built as guard house or 'Covenanter Guard' or, at least the lower section of one, can still be seen in a field opposite Oakwood to the south of Allanton and is now being used as a form of field shed.

*R*everend John Blackadder was arrested in 1681 before being incarcerated on the Bass Rock. By 1685, he had taken seriously ill and was told he would be released provided he lived out his life in Edinburgh but sadly one of Scotland's greatest, and bravest men, died in prison and was buried in the old kirkyard at North Berwick.

*P*erhaps however, Allanbank is most for famous the legend of 'Pearlin Jean' a lady Robert Steuert met in Paris as he was completing his tour of celebration of his 'passing out as a gentleman', something carried out by the many of the gentry in the 17th and 18th centuries. During his stay, he met a lady whom he knew as Jeanne or Jean. Soon they fell in love even though she was said to be a nun, a Sister of Charity; their affair carried on for some time until he was summoned to return to Scotland. As he entered his carriage, a weeping Jean

~ *Allanbank* ~

swept forward begging Robert to stay but the disenchanted 'gentleman' ordered his coachman to drive on, knocking Jean to the ground with a rear wheel rolling over her head, leaving her for dead as Robert demanded the coachman whip up the horses and go even faster. If he thought he had seen the last of Jean, he was mistaken. She arrived at Allanbank before the lord, sitting above the entrance arch 'bidding him welcome home', her head and shoulders covered in blood. For nearly two centuries, Jean, of the pearl laced dress, became the dreaded spectre no one wished to meet.

The old house was later demolished and a new one built during the 18th century meaning the troubled wanderings of the poor Jeanne came to an end. Allanbank was then sold in 1847, to the Houston, later Houston-Boswall Baronets, family who already owned Blackadder House. Allanbank was then used as the Blackadder Dower House but was finally demolished in 1969. Now, the site, only yards to the east of Tofthill, lies bare but the good news is, a new house, known simply as Allanbank, is about to be built on the site of the original house on lands formerly owned by Tofthill Farm, meaning an historic site will once again be a home but without, I'm glad to say, Pearlin' Jean. Happily the old stables, quarters and walled garden of Allanbank remain, giving us all a little insight in to the importance and affluence of a family long departed.

The stables were originally built by Sir John Steuart, between 1760 and 1780 in the shape of a 'U' alongside the magnificent walled garden. The building was fashioned in a French style which Sir John had admired so much during his travels. The 'U' shape was later enclosed, probably in 1820 by the last of the Steuarts, Sir John James, who wished to form a quadrangle, in the same style, around an atmospheric courtyard. Other old houses still exist nearby, including the refurbished old boat house, where once the ferry crossed the river, stands alongside a modern villa. The old farm house still overlooks the steading which is set between the old mill house and the magnificent modern, Allanbank House. That mill steading and the owners, Pauline Burbridge and Charlie Poulsen of **Allanbank Mill Steading (across)** takes us nicely to part one of the Allanbank arts and crafts 'society'

The couple have transformed what was an almost derelict farm steading in to a home, studios and a garden full of sculpture, still and living. Where once stood stables, hayloft, granary, machinery and tractor shed, a dairy, a packing station, byre, egg station and sawmill, there now exists a home, several studios, open cartels and sculpture stores. Sculptures can be seen all around whether in stone, or living plants, it really is a heavenly piece of land where dreams can be realised thanks to Charlie's imagination and skilful hands. For Pauline's part, she is an expert in all things textile and, while she specialises in quilt making to every design imaginable, there are many more strings to her bow. She has had her work exhibited in many fine venues across the country

~ Allanbank ~

including the Albert and Victoria Museum in London. The couple have recently published a book on their projects and growth at the Steading in the first 21 years. Charlie's work consists of all forms of sculpture including what we would regard as 'normal' sculpture as well as studio, drawing and growing, as in all forms of plants. His wonderful creations can be seen all around the steading and really are works of the very highest order, of genius, and a delight to witness. Because his artistic ouput goes much deeper than my words can properly describe, it would be so much better ro attend one of the exhibitions and witness first hand. His works, as are Pauline's, truly are creations of the highest quality and a privilege to witness.

The couple have hosted an exhibition every year since 1994 attracting many enthusiasts and of course, potential customers. They are also teachers of their undoubted talents and all are welcome to their home, studios and most wonderful garden in a steading once the domain of the Turnbull family, one of the many old farming families of the area. We have seen part one of the Allanbank arts fraternity, now it is time to reach out for the old courtyard passing the old entrance to Allanbank and the gateway to Tofthill on the way.

Mike and Liz Hardy have owned Allanbank courtyard for some years and have now transformed the small estate in to a holiday destination, an art studio and a music studio. So much work has been undertaken to transform the old stables and credit must be given to the couple for all their hard work...and talents. Their site includes, the main, quadrangle house with a lovely courtyard in the middle, three holiday cottages and the sublime, modern, Artists' House.

Liz is a multi talented, professional artist and a qualified teacher on the subject and classes are held regularly at Allanbank. She has had a wonderful career which continues at her own piece of paradise in the heart of the Merse. All are welcome to attend her classes regardless of what stage of art they have reached...there is even an art exhibition held annually in the Artists' House. Many other courses are offered including music by Mike who is a professional

~ *Allanbank – Broomdykes* ~

and has played all genres of music from jazz to classical; Mike also conducts lessons at schools and nurseries. Those are but a selection of relaxing pastimes and pursuits though other courses too are on offer. The small estate is a place of great beauty offering a form of peace rarely found in the modern age with so many varieties of trees and shrubs all around, overlooking the most peaceful walks. Adjacent to the courtyard is the magnificent walled garden with an original hexagonal greenhouse on show along with many more glasshouses adorning the old wall. Three beautiful buildings populate the garden including the Garden House overlooking a scene of stunning beauty. All a lifetime away from the days of busy comings and goings and the tragic meanderings of Pearlin' Jeanne.

No matter where we travel throughout life, there is always something, waiting just around the corner, to surprise and delight. During my journey around Duns and the surrounding area, I turned that corner when I arrived at alluring Allanbank, surely a place where dreams are dreamed and really do come true.

Through the arch to the courtyard of Allanbank

~ *Broomdykes* ~

The old Free Kirk of Allanton and the Covenanters' Guard were mentioned earlier as being situated at the junction of the Broomdykes and Allanton roads, let us head east along that road and take a look at one the oldest farms in the district where ancient history is all around the wonderful 19th century farm steading complete with an atmospheric chimney stack. Apart from a fine farmhouse, there are many homes to the east and west forming a little farm town all of its own. The houses, particularly to the west are relatively new but have been built in a very tasteful fashion and so very 'easy on the eyes' The homes to the east have been largely, part of the an old, atmospheric farm

~ *Broomdykes* ~

complex situated in a more than interesting locale.

Quite apart from the old farm buildings, the houses, new and old, the one aspect which shoots out and hits us all between the eyes, is the well kept steading and so clean. From end to end, the entire environ must be a veritable pride and joy to the farmer and his staff and the others who reside nearby. Broomdykes really is joy and a credit to all.

**Above : Broomdykes Farm – The road through and the old stack
Below : Beautiful Silverwood House**

Courtesy of Maggie Maan

~ *Bonkyl and Preston with Lintlaw* ~

*I*t is entirely possible, in times long ago, Bonkyl, while never large, would be a thriving hamlet, situated between its ancient church and castle. It is generally a fact, where there was a castle, a community would grow in the shadow of the walls, for two reasons; one for the obvious safety a castle provided and the other being, many of the villagers owed their livelihood to their master on the other side of the great walls. Of course, where a settled community existed, a church was sure to arrive and there are no reasons whatsoever not to believe there was a stable settlement there, perhaps as old as the one at Dunse Law but Bonkyl is a difficult case, was there a village near the kirk or not? So many pointers suggest there was but they are indeed, rather vague. We do know there has been a church at Bonkill since, at least the late 11th century evidenced by the ancient chancel apse in the kirkyard, perhaps, even earlier and, of course, we know of the early lords and castle but nothing, or very scant indicators, about an actual village.

*B*onkyl has been noted in various spellings over the centuries be it the church, castle, 'village' or parish, everyone appeared to have a different spelling depending on the particular dialect they used. Forgive me for continuing to use the varying spellings as they appeared in any given documents.

*L*ike many areas of Scotland, Bonkill was granted to a knight of Norman descent, during the tenure of the Royal House of Dunkeld; that knight and his family assumed the name 'de Bonkill' in keeping with the times. The church, which was soon to follow, was granted by the king to Dunkeld Abbey as was the church at Preston, the only churches in Berwickshire to be granted to the Perthshire Divine. The first of the de Bonkills was Alexandre, or Alexander, who built the castle (and jail) the scant ruins of which can still be seen, and a tower at Billie. Alexander's daughter and heiress, Margaret, married John Stewart, son of the High Steward of Scotland who inherited the lands of the parish and, during his tenure, it's believed, Bunkle began to grow. Margaret's son fought during the Wars of Independence alongside William Wallace and, ultimately, his future king, Robert de Brus. Her husband, John however, died on the fields of Falkirk in Wallace's fateful defeat. John Stewart of Bonkill was granted the earldom of Angus, following the forfeiture of the de Umfraville family, and the care and maintenance of the barony remained with his family for centuries. Bearing in mind, through the marriage of Marjorie Bruce to the 5th High Steward, their first son, Robert went on to be Robert II of Scots making the Stewarts of Bonkill, cousins of the king such, in that sense at least, expressed the importance of the castle, kirk and lands.

*I*n earlier times, the parish had another connection with the royals of Scotland when the abbot of Dunkeld, Ethelred, was said to have visited both Bunkle and Preston. Ethelred was not only Abbot, he was also a royal prince, the son of Malcolm III and the brother of four kings, Duncan, Edgar,

~ *Bonkyl* ~

Alexander and David, all ascending the throne of Scotland while Ethelred chose an ecclesiastical vocation. The visit of Ethelred to Bunkle would probably be as much political as it was ecclesiastical. The House of Dunkeld cherished their great footholds in the south and Berwickshire was especially vital to their survival. It was less than a century since the treaty at Carham in 1013, that the lands of Berwickshire were, from that moment on, officially, not part of Northumbria but it would take so much longer for the House of Dunkeld to gain the trust of the people.

Some years later, David I, was called on to intervene in a controversy which had raged for some time, of where the boundary line was between Coldinghamscire and Bonkillscire and though the argument was settled, William I, David's grandson, was called some years later to settle the same problem, he may even have visited his Bon Clll. *The Chapel at the foot of the ridge,* a very apt description considering the church's situation.

Of course kings were not the only men we know of at Bunkle, mentions of many of the local dignitaries have been handed down to us over the years. During his reign as Sheriff of Berwick in the1180s, Adam de Bunkle had to arbitrate in a case between Bertram the prior of Durham and his counterpart at Coldingham Priory; Ralph of Bunkle was mentioned even earlier, before, in 1203, Arnold, prior of Coldingham was witness to a toft of land in Coldingham, which had been sold by Alexander de Bunkle. Between 1211 and 1228AD, many mentions were made of Alexander de Bonkil, in charters including his attendance at the wedding of Alexander II to Joan of England. John of Bunkle was mentioned as being the chaplain of Bunkle between 1214 and 1221 while in 1225, another chaplain, who was also a canon of Dunkeld, was mentioned simply as 'A' of Bunkle.

More included John of Bunkle who, in 1244, was a juror at a case which involved Patrick, Earl of Dunbar and Earl Walter Comyn of Menteith. In 1283, William of Bunkle granted lands at Rottenrow in Glasgow to the Corporation of that city before, in 1286, John Stewart was appointed as an auditor to Robert Bruce of Carrick, the future king, before joining Wallace during the 'Great Cause' fighting bravely at Stirling in 1297 before, as we have seen, dying at Falkirk barely a year later. Hemmed between those dates, John, brother of James, High Steward of Scotland, swore fealty to Edward I in 1296 as did Thomas, the Master of Bunkle in the company of John, Agnes and Nicolas Perre, all designated 'of Bunkle' – a very important locale indeed.

Many castles were built in Berwickshire in those early times but they were needed because of the constant threat from the south and fortresses at Bunkle and nearby Billie and Blanerne were crushed during the *'Wars of the Rough Wooing'* in 1544-46 as Hertford's forces destroyed everything in sight during their mauling of southern Scotland. That was the most barbaric period in Scotland's history caused by a brutal megalomaniac, Henry VIII. Henry

~ *Bonkyl* ~

wanted everything around him, he was bound by no law other then is own 'self esteem' Anything and everything, in his evil opinion, was his!

*A*n old rhyme of the day, referring to David I and the castles mentioned after their destructions, reads as follows :

> *Buncle, Billie and Blanairne*
> *Three castles strong as airn*
> *Built when Davy wis a bairn*
> *They'll a' gang doon*
> *Wi Scotland's Croon*
> *An ilka ane will be a cairn*

Ruins of Bunkle Castle
Courtesy of Lisa Jarvis - Geograph

*T*hat act of wanton destruction would result in the decline of any settlement which may have existed but the decline would be indeed slow, since there is evidence of a small settlement in to, at least, the early 19th century. What is not clear is, if the settlement was grouped or scattered around the parish.

*T*he local people were gainfully employed in the fields and probably weaving and quarrying, there is known to have been blacksmiths, joiners and a tailor too at the settlement. Digs, some of which have already taken place when a 12th century coin was found, will continue in the near future to establish the whereabouts of the elusive village. If nothing else, hopefully, it will throw more light on the matter.

*B*y 1660, Bunkle Kirk was in serious decline and much of the fabric of the building was terribly decayed. It was decided to move the congregation to nearby Preston Church but the synod soon had a change of heart, carried out great renovation and renewal, allowing the church to live on but alas, Preston, was allowed to die, the sad ruins of which can still be seen in old Preston kirkyard. Part of their change of heart was, "the larger congregation still existed near the church of Bunkle" while Preston was smaller than it is today. A little more evidence of a settlement near the kirk? Further repairs were carried out at Bonkyl in 1716 before a total rebuild just over a century later.

*T*he new church was built in 1820, using the stone from the older kirk, in a plain rectangular style with a vestibule added to the west, so typical of many

~ *Bonkyl* ~

19th century country kirks. The classical belfry, situated at the west gable, is home to a bell of 1728. The present building is possibly the third perhaps even the fourth, on the site since late 11th century as evidenced in the Norman doorway to the ancient apse at the south side of the kirk. That doorway is believed to be from the first kirk which was thought to have been built by the same masons who built Jedburgh Abbey; the arch leads to the burial aisle of the Homes of Billie. The last burial, in 1751, was that of Lady Margaret (Billie) Home who was murdered by her butler Norman Ross when she caught him red-handed attempting to steal. Ross was hanged at Edinburgh after having his right hand cut off. Lady Margaret was mother to Patrick Home who built the grand house of Paxton.

    Duns architect, George Fortune was commissioned to restore and renovate the kirk in 1905 and the finished product is legacy to his genius. He altered and

Left :
Bonkyl Kirk
with the
ancient apse,
The Billie Burial Ground
to the right

Below :
The Chancel

restored much of the Romanesque-style church and, to the west, added a rectangular crow-stepped porch and vestry topped by a cross finial to the south gable apex. Before Fortune's work, Bunkle Church was described as being a rectangular barn-like structure and if it was not for the belfry, could never have been mistaken for a church.

    The porch, with wheelchair access, is dado panelled with doors leading to the vestry and nave with steps leading to the loft while lancet, stained glass windows are situated to the east and west. On entering the nave we are met with a central aisle splitting two sections of stained pews and facing the most glorious sight of a Norman style chancel arch with two, tall round head,

~ Bonkyl – Lintlaw ~

stained glass windows featuring the Lord and the Virgin Mary. The light embraces the carved communion table topped by a brass lectern and sided by five chairs. The wide spaces to each side of the chancel are hidden behind four columned blind arcades.

The pulpit is on the east end of the north wall and the organ opposite on the south. The octagonal timber font stands alongside a tall pine lectern which was dedicated to the memory of a local lady, Helen Logan. Two round head windows centred by two arched bipartite windows add much light over the nave from the south. Viewed from the outside, the windows, enclosed by sublime columned arches, are works of genius. The lower section of the walls are covered with timber dado panelling below cream coloured, plastered walls and flat ceiling. Converted oil lamps, suspended from the ceiling, light up the church in darker moments. The tiered gallery above the west end of the nave, supported by two white metal columns, adds to the overall seating capacity and it is not difficult to understand why beautiful Bonkyl Kirk is such a popular venue for weddings amidst the most peaceful settings. The little church at the foot of the ridge, the pathetic ruins of the castle with a few buildings joining the old Manse and the houses at nearby Marygold, are all that is left. If a village did indeed exist at Bunkle, the dwellings would almost certainly be of wood meaning, when the settlement was finally abandoned, the cottages would disappear almost without trace, perhaps in the early to mid 19th century.

.~ Lintlaw ~

Nearby Lintlaw, still survives and flourishes at, what can best be described, as a little 'farm toun' where once all the children of the entire parish attended

school. The last schoolhouse opened in 1860 but closed in more recent times due to falling rolls, so endemic of rural areas in the modern age. That school,

~ *Lintlaw – Preston* ~

which is now a private home, known as Bunkle House. succeeded another place of education which was situated a little to the south-east, though it is almost certain a school would exist near the old kirk of Bunkle and may well have opened, perhaps within a few years of the Reformation of 1560.

The owners of Lintlaw Farm, the Calder family, are related to the late and great Jim Clark and he was a 'weel kent' face around the hamlet for many years and where he garaged his Lotus rally cars. The farm itself is a very well kept affair and a great credit to the owners and farm hands. A curiosity stands, fitted on a wall on the opposite side of the cottages, which looks for all the world like an old range fireplace, with a coal basket which is a true work of iron art in its own right.

Lintlaw is a lovely wee place in which to live, with several fine old cottages, a few new houses and a splendid farmhouse. Lovely walks are situated all around the well kept farm and hamlet and though there are no shops nor facilities, the people have only a few minutes drive to and from Chirnside, meaning the kids don't have far to travel for school nor the parents for their shopping.

~ *Preston* ~

Still part of the old parish, Preston in the present day, is the only settlement in the area worthy of the title 'village' Today's hamlet is a quiet place but is an intensely proud community with a wonderful village hall where many activities, including social gatherings, take place and where the members of Berwickshire Hunt Supporters Club congregate on occasion. The village contains an old market cross signifying more important days of yesteryear when the small cottage shops of the 19th century, water mills, small weaving industry and the local school thrived. Like many other small villages and parishes in Scotland, yesterday's prosperity has all but gone but, against all the odds, Preston still sits proud on the principal Duns to Grantshouse road.

Just to the south-east of the village stands the Monument to de la Bastie, erected in remembrance of the murder of the French Knight, Antoine Dargie de la Bastie of whom we learned of earlier. To get to that monument, we must cross the Nell Logan Bridge across the Preston Burn as it flows to wards the greater waters of Lady Whiteadder. That bridge is particularly interesting, or should be said, a section under the single arch bridge, which was enclosed to form a jail during the Napoleonic Wars to detain French prisoners of war before they were moved to more secure units. The prison bridge is so called since the famous Nell was the last prisoner held in the small jail, her crime? stealing sheep, a crime which has immortalised her name in local folklore, locked between the cold waters and the road to Hammerhall, another of the parish's little farm settlements where the principal blacksmith was kept busy.

~ *Preston* ~

As we have seen, many ancient sites exist around the area of the old parish with the previously mentioned Buncle, Blanerne and Billie castles, but one of the more recent notable structures is Bonkyl Lodge, an atmospheric country house built by the 12th Earl of Home in the latter part of the 19th century.

Preston's main street, though dominated by the farm, boasts some interesting homes like the Old Schoolhouse which stands as a sentinel opposite the War Memorial Cross, while another interesting building is the Old Farm House, where guests are welcomed for Bed and Breakfast. That is not to say they are the only two but what strikes the visitor loud and clear, is the lovely blend of housing whether social and private, old and new. The farm of course, reminds us of the origins of the village and proving 'King Agriculture' still has a roll to play in modern society. Let us not forget the ancient Cross which stands to the north of the through road, broken but unsullied.

The Village Hall

The Mercat Cross
courtesy of Walter Baxter

The remains of the 12th century Preston Church are situated to the south-west of the village down the Kirk Brae. Like Bonkyl, the old church was in the see of Dunkeld Abbey until the Reformation, and served the parish until closure in 1718 when it fell in to long term decay. The church, nave and chancel, was an especially large church for its day and the sorry remains can still be seen, situated on the knoll above the present day cemetery and overlooking the everlasting Whiteadder and is well worthy of a visit.

The ruins are especially substantial mainly due to the many family burial grounds built within. The north wall needed some remedial works in recent times to prevent collapse but has saved a very fine ruin of a very fine church, for future generations to view and admire.

~ *Preston* ~

*W*e know of some names from early times though not so many as Bunkle however the following were mentioned in charters of the early years; those included Robert of Preston who was a canon of Dunkeld in the early 1200s, Lawrence of Preston who swore fealty to Edward of England in 1296 and William of Preston who was known to be a servant to Richard Bromsgrove, who was a canon of the 14th century. Of the village itself, not so much is known despite its antiquity. We do know of a school and a later school at Millburn to the west; a small home grocery and several of the trades concerned with the country and farm but no tell of an inn. What is certain though, the parish boasted one of the great mills of the Borders, the great Cumledge Mill, the biggest employer in the area. While the beautiful whitewashed housing is still intact, the wonderful old mill has gone the way of so many others in the never ending cycle of centralisation and foreign imports.

*T*he first mention of Cumledge, as far as anyone knows, arrived in the early 15th century when it was mentioned in *'The Book of Charter'* before, in 1431, when there is tell of the proprietor, George Sleigh of Culleyg (Cumledge) Further notes are made of the *Waulke Mill of Cumledge* in the early 1700s.

Above :

Ruins of Preston Church

Left :

The Houses at Cumledge Mill

119

~ *Preston - Chirnside* ~

The mill changed ownership several times over the years and produced so many different types of material but finally opted for blankets. In that niche trade, it survived and prospered but when the great wars erupted twice in the 20th century, the mill owners were instructed to produce the materials required for army clothing. After the 2nd World War, Cumledge returned to blankets but disaster struck in 1948 and the great floods when so much was simply washed away, an event which was experienced all over Berwickshire. The housing and mill were devastated but after a great deal of hard work and effort, the mill was back in business but never to the same levels as before. Sadly, in 1972, the Cumledge Mill closed for the last time. One of the great pages in Berwickshire's history had closed forever and while most of the housing still stands, the magnificent mill is no more but will live on, in the annals of Preston forever.

Notable people associated with the parish as a whole are, John Brown M.D., (1735-88) founder of the Brunonian system of medicine, was born in Bunkle while Dr James Hutton of nearby Slighshouses Farm introduced the Norfolk system of drill husbandry between 1754 and 1768.

~ *Chirnside – Chirnsidebridge* ~

The name 'Chirnside' is said to be derived from '*The Sepulchral Tumulus on the side of the hill*' or more commonly *Cairn on the side of the hill.* A cairn which is said to have covered the grave of a great warrior but sadly, the site of the Cairn, on nearby Harelaw, was cleared in 1906 to create a reservoir. From the beginning, the settlement was of some importance and, though never growing to any great degree, maintained that importance until well beyond the Reformation of the Church in 1560.

Chirnside Parish Church was founded during the reign of King Edgar in the first decade of the 12th century though there are others who believe a divine place of worship was erected there in the first half of the 7th century but, unfortunately that cannot be substantiated. Even so, considering its situation in the south-east, and it's former importance as a Presbytery which contained more than a dozen other parishes including Berwick, it is entirely possible a place of worship would be established in early times. The first church was a long rectangular building of stone, earthen floor and thatched roof and, while the date of that church is not entirely clear, sections of the present structure are from the 12th century. The patronage of the kirk was in the hands of the Earls of Dunbar until their temporary demise in the 15th century.

The earliest preacher to be recorded at the church in the Deanery of the Merse was Symon, Parsonna de Chyrnsyde who prospered in his calling, at a place endowed by the Gospatrick earls of Dunbar. William de Blyda, a

~ Chirnside ~

successor to Symon, had the dubious pleasure of swearing fealty to Edward I at Berwick in 1296. The church went from strength to strength and, on the 10th April 1242, was consecrated by David de Bernham, the celebrated Bishop of St. Andrews. The Reverend David was an extremely busy man, consecrating no less than 140 churches in the 1240s. Later, in 1342, when the Collegiata Ecclessia de Sancta Bae de Dunbar was founded by Patrick of Dunbar, Chyrnsyde was erected as a prebend of the great collegiate church, the first such church in the region. Though the forming of the prebendary status arrived in 1342, connections with Dunbar Church stretched back to the 12th century as evidenced by the Dunbars' patronage and many land transactions which took place between the two establishments.

It would appear, over the years there were many disputes, claims and quitclaims over lands which were gifted or taken as the case may be. In several instances, the procurator of Melrose Abbey was summoned to settle disputes. In one particular case on Monday, 1st April, 1291, Adam of Fogo, brother and procurator of Melrose, decided against Patrick of Lemmington, Rector of Dunbar who had claimed ownership of lands and houses around Chirnside and several areas in Haddingtonshire. Patrick is said to have been the parson at Chirnside before his 'elevation' to the Rectory of Dunbar. Other names from early times included landowners William and Alice de Chyrnsyde who gifted much land to the church at various points between 1250 and 1270, Mariota, who would appear to be of the Swinton family who with her son, Patrick, was responsible for more gifts of land. Others known with connection to the church were Simon in the mid 13th century and Hugh in the very early 14th century.

Towards the end of the 15th century, decisions were taken to build fortifications with lookout points at and around the church because of ever ongoing raids from the south as we have so often seen at other villages around Duns. During the 16th century, the attacks were intensified particularly during the Rough Wooing Wars and the local dignitaries were prepared for more, meaning there was always someone on

Chirnside Parish Church

~ *Chirnside* ~

lookout duty from the kirk or the nearby tower. One, night a young local man, Luke Anderson, was on watch from the tower when several men approached menacingly - they were English freebooters looking for a 'quick gain'. When Luke descended the tower to approach them, they had disappeared and, as the lad tried to raise the alarm, they surged forward from behind bushes and murdered him, no one was ever apprehended but still the watch continued but from that point, there was always more than one sharing the vigil.

*T*he church was damaged at the Reformation and was largely rebuilt in 1573 before being repaired in the 17th century and extensively enlarged in the early 19th century while further large scale alterations were undertaken in 1878. In 1904, following the death of Lady Tweedmouth, her husband, Edward, funded a complete renovation of the church including the building of the tower, vestry, porch, belfry, laird's aisle and church hall to designs by Arthur Mitchell and George Wilson. When Edward Marjoribanks, 2nd Baron Tweedmouth died, his son bought two cottages near the church, demolished them and built a wonderful gateway **(below)** as a memorial to his father.

*T*he church building as we have seen retains much of the original 12th century structure including an arch above the south-west door from the late Norman period. There is no doubt, considering various differing styles of the exterior building work, there are several sections from a much earlier church or churches, complete with masons' marks. The present church, before the Marjoribank 20th century extension work, was a simple rectangle Romanesque style building with the belfry at the west gable - a typical early Scottish Kirk. The additions give an appearance of extravaganza but nothing can blemish the beauty of the church, exterior and interior.

*T*he 'T' plan of the interior (nave and north transcept) of an irregular shaped exterior, contains carpeted, boarded flooring with some slabs, much timber dado panelling embellishes the walls which are otherwise of cream coloured plaster. A platform on the south wall supports the extraordinarily high, octagonal pulpit, stone font and communion table. There is an old stone in the interior of the south wall with the inscription 'Helpe the Pvr - 1573'. Help the Poor! - such powerful words, and just as meaningful now, more than 400 years later as they were then.

~ *Chirnside* ~

Chyrneside was regarded by King James VI as one of his special Presbyteries and was thought to have visited on more than one occasion. As it happens, James did make a point of visiting all the prebendary churches of Dunbar Collegiate Church.

The first minister in the wake of the Reformation was Rev. John Home but like the parson at Duns was actually known as the Rector which probably had something to do with Collegiate Church at Dunbar. A little later, in 1578, the Rev. Thomas Storie was the first, fully ordained, reformed minister at the kirk; The present minister is Rev. Bruce Neill, who has recently been handed the ancient charge.

A 17th century minister of the church was the Rev. Henry Erskine who was imprisoned during covenanting times for his refusal to adhere to the Anglican prayer book which had been forced upon the established church in Scotland and is buried in the kirkyard. Both his sons were ministers and one of them, Ebeneezer, with others, broke from the kirk to establish the Secession Church because of differing opinions within the assembly of the church. Later, the Secession Church split into Burgher and anti-Burgher factions. In 1847, a now United Secession Church joined the Relief Church to form the United Presbyterian Church of Scotland. Both Ebeneezer and his brother Ralph, are forever remembered as two of Scotland's greatest ministers.

A Cameronian or Reformed Presbyterian Church was built in 1783 at the top of the Cross Hill on the main junction within the village but has long since closed and is now used as the community centre. It is thought, the Rev. James Purves, the eminent Scottish Universalist Minister was a member of the congregation during their days of worship in the fields and farm sheds in the years before the kirk was built. Another kirk, a United Presbyterian, situated behind the houses on the Main Street opposite the community centre, was opened in 1857 and named the Erskine Memorial. That church was later used as a hall, the Comrades Hall, but has been demolished to make way for a Church of Scotland sheltered housing complex. There was also a Gospel Hall on Main Street in the late 19th and in to the 20th century but that has long since been converted to a private flat. In the present day, only the Parish Kirk exists joined by Southview Evangelical Church situated at Crosshill opposite the community centre. Other denominations in the village, each only for a relatively short time were, Methodists and an Episcopal Mission from Duns.

Agriculture has always played a big part in village life, and still does, with all the trades, associated with the farms present. Specialised paper making too has played a huge part in the welfare of the village people having been manufacturing since the 18th century but more of that at Chirnsidebridge. Another successful business near the village is a large sawmill which is situated a little to the south on the Allanton Road.

Chirnside contains most of what is required required for day to day living

~ *Chirnside* ~

though it has to be said, the people must still travel for larger shops either to Duns or Berwick but that was not always the case. In times long gone, Chirnside, was fairly well self sufficient and during the earlier part of the 19th century, a very impressive list of shops and trades were in place, let's take a look. Between 1825 and 1837, there existed a library, gas company, three inns, eight grocers, two butchers, four bakers, paper mill, two sawmills, sack and linen weavers, four shoe and boot makers, five drapers, tailors, two ironmongers, cattle dealers, millwrights, joiners and carpenters, slaters, saddlers, blacksmiths, two children's nurseries, maltings and a brewery along with all the other trades required of a rural country community. What we have to remember however is, several of the 'shops' may have been inside people's homes perhaps selling at the back door but by no means all.

Left :

**The old school
Courtesy
of
Mark Kinghorn**

Below :

**The primary school
of
today**

*D*uring that period of course, there were still four 'working' churches including the Gospel Hall and three schools, the Parish, Ninewells School and a girls only school.

~ *Chirnside* ~

*L*ater inventories give us a much clearer indications of what businesses existed in the village when there were two butcher shops, a chemist, a confectioner, five grocers and one grocer/draper, two tearooms, two bakers, drapers, ironmongers, post office, police station and doctor's surgery. There was also a bank, two inns, the Red Lion and the Waterloo. There were other traders of course but that gives a more balanced indication of more 'modern' times in the village and how busy it was. There was also the bowling green, football pitches, tennis courts as there is today, and so many fine walks. While many of the facilities have gone, many are still with us today.

*T*here is still some work in and around the village, like the paper industry as we shall see, the aforementioned sawmill, garage services and shops but again, for many, travel is required for gainful employment but no longer by train since the local station closed in 1951 for passengers but for freight it was more than ten years later. Having said that, never believe Chirnside is a back water, far from it, and there is so much going on. It still boasts a well respected primary school contained in an art-deco building of 1937, designed by architects, Reid and Forbes. Many clubs exist including a bowling club, football club, youth activities at the Community Centre most evenings, a boxing club, Scottish Women's Rural Institute, a History Club, Development Group who organise many activities like concerts, coffee mornings then there is the following impressive list of other activities and groups like regular concerts, MS Society, Toddlers and Senior Citizen groups, a very long standing Horticultural Society, WRVS and the Scottish Borders Youth Voice. WRI and Women's Guild. Those groups and activities are joined by so many more including nearby stables where all are welcome. Youngsters too are well looked after and, apart from Toddlers Groups and Nurseries, there are clubs for the Beavers, Rainbows, Brownies and Cubs and, as mentioned, there are some shops, a nice selection too. Eating out is well catered for around the region as is take away meals while nearby hotels and guest houses look after every visitor's needs. All the clubs and societies come together for the village's greatest week of the year, the *Chirnside Civic Week* which is held in June. The principals of the week are the Gala Queen and her Consort who were in 2015, Hannah Black and Nicholas Warnock respectively. The great event begins with the *Kirkin's o' the Queen* at the Parish Kirk before the toastin' then the official crowning at the Windram Park.

*T*here are festivities and events held over the next week including the Carnival, fancy dress parade, bingo in one of the inns, a mile race at the football park, bowling competition, a pet show, kids' bingo and adult quiz night. The festivities came to an end in 2015, when a party and fancy dress ball was held in the Robin's Nest Inn with everyone fully in the party mood after a wonderfully enjoyable week.

*T*he three big houses of Chirnside are sadly no longer homes; Ninewells,

~ *Chirnside* ~

the childhood home of the inimitable David Hume, was demolished in 1954, Whitehall, once a home of the prominent Halls of Dunglass family, was demolished in 2015 after lying derelict for some years and, finally, Maines House which was converted to a fine hotel, Chirnside Hall. That house of the mid 19th century was occupied for several years by James Grant-Suttie the 'to be' Baronet of Balgone and Prestongrange in East Lothian. Interestingly, the beautiful lodges of those old houses can still be viewed and admired.

There have been many notable men of Chirnside including of course, the Erskine family of ministers but two men of the village who achieved lasting, world wide acclaim, were David Hume and Jim Clark.

David Hume was born in Edinburgh on 7th May, 1711, to Chirnside parents but received his early education in Chirnside after his parents moved back to Ninewells when he was a child. At the age of 12, he studied at Edinburgh University before going on to be one of the greatest academics of his day and was very prominent during the era of the Scottish Enlightenment.

Right :
Whitehall Manor
David Lauder 2007 –
Wikipedia

Below :
Chirnside Hall Hotel
formerly Maines House
John Whelan 2007 - Geograph

He was born David Home but changed the spelling of his surname to Hume when English people continued to mispronounce Home. He was a philosopher and his most famous work on the subject was *The Treatise of Human Nature* written when he was only 28 years old. He was one of Scotland's greatest academics and while a brilliant pupil of the school of Scottish Enlightenment, he most certainly was a teacher of Naturalism, several areas of philosophy and Liberalism amongst many other genres. He was a prolific writer and one of his most read works was the six volume *History of England,* but that was only one of so many works he compiled over the years. He died in 1776 at the grand old age (for that time) of 65 and was buried in the town in which he was born, Edinburgh in the Calton Hill cemetery where a

~ Chirnside ~

great mausoleum was erected over his grave.

While a hero of the Scottish Academia, he was also a very humble man who set out on a mission while still a child at Chirnside Parochial School. That mission was duly completed and still he remains a hero and a much loved man, one of the greatest ever to wear the tag "I am a Scot" He, like Scott, Burns, Fleming, Smith and so many more, was a 'product' of the Scottish education system which was envied the world over and the pride of all Scots.

We have read of Jim Clark's achievements in the Duns section but to the people of Chirnside, he is one of their bairns. He was born at Kilmany in Fife but moved with the family when they took over Edington Mains Farm near Chirnside and it was on that farm he learned to drive, the rest on that score, as they say, is history. He was educated the Chirnside Primary before moving on to Clifton Hall School in Edinburgh then Loretto School at Musselburgh. He was though, often spotted in the village and truly was 'a local lad' who made good. His career is legend and it is no exaggeration to say, he was the world's greatest ever racing driver at that time. Had he not been plucked from us at such a young age, there is no telling what he could have gone on to achieve.

The great man died in Hockenheim in 1968 and was buried in Chirnside Kirkyard. A wonderful clock monument has been raised in his honour and memory at Crosshill in the village, he indeed was a *Flower of Scotland* and we may never see his like again but his achievements will live forever.

There is so much to see around Chirnside and what better way to witness such a lovely area than to take and enjoy some of the many fine walks around the village, walks which were probably enjoyed by David Hume as a youngster including the old doo'cot of Ninewells and the walkway around his childhood home before following on the banks of the Whiteadder Water for some distant witnessing so many wonderful views on the way. Other walks are available including a circular walk which includes the tiny hamlet of Chirnsidebridge to the west. On our way to the hamlet, we pass Ninewells Farm, surely one of the best kept steadings in the Borders.

**Left :
Southfield
Evangelical
Church**

~ *Chirnside* ~

After more than 900 years of recorded history, Chirnside continues to thrive and the many new houses which have been, and are continuing to be built, will ensure the lovely village overlooking the Merse has a long and bright future.

Before leaving Chirnside, though, it is important to mention Edington a little to the south-east of the village, where Jim Clark grew up. Apart from his father's farm, Edington Mains, there was the tiny hamlet at Edington Mill further south on the Whiteadder Water. In the modern day the settlement at the Mill is bludgeoning with many of the old mill buildings being converted and so many new houses being built forming a formidable community amidst the most pleasing environs but community to this area is no stranger and there is thought to have been a village around Edington Bastle since the 11th century. The Bastle was thought to have been destroyed during the 'Rough Wooing' sorties of the 16th century

The Jim Clark Memorial Clock

before a more modern castle was built surrounded by a moat. The remains of the castle, or what is left of them, can still be seen but the moat is no longer visible. Still the construction of so many houses on the lands of Edington ensures a continuity of community which has lasted at least 1,000 years

Above : Building works at Edington Mill overlooking the old mill lade
©2013 Barbara Carr - Geograph

~ *Chirnsidebridge* ~

The 'village centre'

Chirnsidebridge is a lovely little hamlet containing many fine houses and a little industry at and near the former railway station and old Chirnside Mill. There is a larger house, Rockcliffe House, in the village, which is found at the end of a driveway leading off the Blanerne/Preston road which passes over another old bridge, the Billieburn Bridge on its way north. Rockcliffe House is owned by the mill owners, Ahlstrom who occupy a site full of fine old industrial buildings, the manager's house and others which once served as workers' homes and, of course, the great mill buildings, all overlooked by the most impressive stack. The old road once crossed a wonderful 18th century bridge which, in the modern day, still stands but is now redundant being replaced by the David Hume Bridge which was erected to take the heavier traffic flow on the road to Duns. At the side of the old bridge, which is raised higher to the east, stands the scant ruins of the famous old Rock House which was built in to the rock of the banking.

The Old Chirnside Bridge with the paper mills behind featuring the historic stack

Courtesy of Walter Baxter Geograph

Chirnsidebridge is best known for paper making, an industry which has been carried out since early times. Indeed, in a publication of Berwick in 1806,

~ *Chirnsidebridge* ~

the mill was referred to thus *"Mr. Robert Blackadder has erected a Paper-Mill at the bridge-end and an elegant house. It is the most delightful situation in Berwickshire, and the improvements he has made are remarkable"* However, that was not the first mill which was erected in 1770. In 1882, the mill was reconstructed for the Young Trotter Company by the architectural and building firm of David Cousin. In the 1930s however, the Dickinson Company owned the mill, a mill which was now producing high quality paper for an array of different products. The great paper mill was later owned by the Dexter Corporation who sold out to Ahlstrom, a Finnish Company in 2000 and still, production goes on merrily as it has done for nearly three centuries.

As we know, the Berwickshire Railway closed to passenger trains in 1951 but the railway buildings at Chirnsidebridge (Chirnside Station) can still be seen. In the old days, the goods wagons stopped at the mill delivering esparto grass and China clay on a near daily basis. All over the Borders, railways were closing, partly due to the great storms of 1948 and partly for no better reason than, they were operating at a loss.

A little to the west of the paper mill stands beautiful Newstead Farm and, beyond, a large potato packing station at Craigswalls. Though situated in the Parish of Edrom, Craigswalls, thankfully, provides jobs for the people of Chirnside.

All set in the most beautiful environs, with the fertile Merse to the south and the rolling hills of the Lammermuirs to the north, the contented people of Chirnside and surrounds are a happy community who never forget to wish a stranger, a warm welcome to their lovely village, one the truly ancient communities of the Merse.

~ *A Lingering Look Back at Chirnside* ~

Old Station Buildings at Chirnside Station
© Ben Brooksbank 1997 Geograph

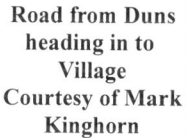

Road from Duns heading in to Village
Courtesy of Mark Kinghorn

The West End

Courtesy of Mark Kinghorn

~ *Cranshaws* ~

*A*lmost replicating the origins of Bunkle, this place which became known as Cranshaws would almost certainly have formed a community before the arrival of a church but possibly in the wake of the building of the first fortress. While the first known mention of Cranshaws Castle is 1350, it is almost certain, some kind of 'power house' was in place much earlier considering its situation on the most important route over the old Lambermora Hills, (Lammermuirs) a route which ran between the most important towns in the extreme south east of Scotland, Duns, Berwick and Haddington. Again, like many other settlements in the region, whatever there was of a village, has all but disappeared though in the case of Cranshaws, there are still a goodly number of houses dotted around near the farm and castle where the old village would exist in days of old, and at the 'new village centre' where also exists the village hall.

*L*ike the castle, It is not entirely clear when the church at Cranshaws was founded but it was certainly well established by 1274 when it was included under the name of Craneshaues in the Bagimund Rolls. Later, the parson, Robert de Strivelin swore fealty to Edward I at Berwick

The Village Hall

in 1296 thus having his rights to the church restored by the evil English king. That early church and its altar, were dedicated to St. Ninian (Scotland's first saint) and it is widely believed the church may have been established, with so many others in south-east Scotland, in the 12th century. What is certain, a church was only planted in the midst of a community therefore it is reasonable to believe, there was already a village in place before 1274. Another chapel is believed to have existed during the Swinton stewardship of the castle, which was situated at or near that family burial ground.

*T*he route on which the village stands, was a busy thoroughfare in times long before the lands were part of what became Scotland. Apart from the pre-historic tribes including the Ottadini, the Romans would no doubt trudge their way through to be followed by the Angles and Saxons busy in their conquest to take lands in to their newly founded kingdom of Northumbria. The last major assault of those early times was that of the Vikings who, having already

~ *Cranshaws* ~

conquered Ireland and much of Cumbria and Northumbria, were hell bent on taking more. So many ancient sites dotted all around, including burial cairns and hillforts, are all testament to very early habitation.

The village and parish are thought to be named after the long-legged bird, the crane or heron and the surrounding woodlands thus the *Crane Wood* or, as it is today, Cranshaws.

The tiny hamlet, sitting on the B6355 nine and half miles north-west of Duns, is one of the highest settlements in the Scottish Borders and is overshadowed by the mighty Dog Law to the west. The present church, a little to the south-east of the original Cranshaws Church and kirkyard, is situated near the right bank of the Whiteadder Water. The old manse is just to the north while the mighty tower-house of Cranshaws with the more gentle Cranshaws House and Farm situated near the ruined kirk.

The original church, of which some remains and broken gravestones can still be seen, was built in what was almost certainly the most populous part of the parish near the castle and the Townhead of Cranshaws. The original castle is thought to pre-date the church and was a stronghold of the powerful Douglas family though it came in to the hands of the prominent Swintons in the first decade of the 15th century which may be a hint as to which family was victorious in 1402 at the Battle of Main (or Man) Slaughter Law when the forces of the powerful families of Douglas and Hepburn of Hailes stood toe to toe in mortal combat; many items of warfare ironmongery have been discovered over the centuries at Mainslaughter Law where a tumulus sits at the summit.

The Swintons held the Barony of Cranshaws for nearly 300 years and, from them, we get an indication to the dedication of the church. The wife of Sir John Swinton, Catherine Lauder, died in 1515, and her sole wish was to be buried in front of the alter at her beloved church of St. Ninian at Cranshaws, perhaps confirming the church was blessed in the name of that saint who is also known as St. Ringan. Some years earlier, in 1476, Sir John had taken out a legal action against John of Ellem regarding a chapel at Cranshaw Castle but the details of the action are not known. On a happier note between the two churches, both were created prebends of the Chapel Royal at Stirling Castle. Perhaps that is the reason we do not find the first minister of the reformed Church of Cranshaws until 1572 when Matthew Liddell was inducted prior to him, the preaching appeared to be shared by the parson, David Swinton and the vicar-pensioner, David Knowes. Perhaps, like other churches in the same situation, like Chirnside and Duns, the prebendary clerics were allowed to stay just a little longer than in independent kirks.

The most memorable (or otherwise) happening at the old church was the visit of King James VI in the 1590s, a notable occasion for more reasons than one. Normally when a monarch decides to visit a church, it is a great honour

~ *Cranshaws* ~

for the whole congregation but this turned out to be one of great embarrassment when the minister, Alexander Swinton of Swinton, forgot to say the normal prayer for the king and was scolded by James in no uncertain manner. The king ordered a plaque be struck to forever remind the minister and congregation of the omission and was placed opposite the pulpit. When the church closed, the plaque was taken in to the new kirk.

*D*avid Denham bought the castle and lairdship in 1702 before gifting it to his son, James Denham but James sold the lands a few years later to James Watson of Saughton near Edinburgh. The castle then passed through Watson's mother's family to the Lord Aberdour, son of the Earl of Morton, thus returning the old fortalice to the Douglas family. Towards the end of the 19th century the castle was purchased by the benevolent Andrew Smith of Whitchester but it was later purchased by Landale family, As a note of interest, in the latter part of the 16th century, the castle was downsized and a new tower house, the present, built in an oblong shape, of rubble stone with harled walls and rounded edges; the tower is 65 feet high and 40 feet x 26 feet in dimension with five feet thick walls helping survive the the worst of the weather and anything else which has been thrown at it. In the modern day the castle is now used as a very upmarket holiday home.

**Cranshaws Castle circa 2006
courtesy of Lisa Jarvis - Geograph**

*T*he first church on the present site was opened in 1739 but the ministers were constantly complaining it was of inferior design and construction causing the need for constant repairs. During the life of that church, a now closed school was built for the children of the parish just to the north of the village hall. Finally, after nearly 160 years of service, the 18th century kirk was demolished making way for the church we now know.

*T*oday's church is described as one of the very few Romanesque revival kirks, of excellent design and construction by George Fortune, a Duns architect, and financed wholly by Andrew Smith of Cranshaws and Whitchester (see Longformacus) a philanthropic local landowner and Edinburgh brewer. Incidentally, George Fortune built the porch as a gift to the

~ *Cranshaws* ~

church. The lovely old kirk sits at the foot of a heavenly dale near the Whiteadder Water and overlooked by trees to the east and west. The building is essentially of rectangular shape with a bowed apse added to the east, a large porch and vestibule to the south-west and a vestry added to an aisle on the north-east. The rubble and red stone dressed building is topped by a grey slated roof with a birdcage bellcote on the west gable.

Cranshaws Kirk courtesy of Walter Baxter

The church is brightened by four round head windows on the south, a round head window with 'Y' shaped central mullion and lovely rose window to the west while the apse contains three beautiful stained glass windows.

The dark stained and elaborately embellished hammer-beamed roof looks down over white walls with lower stained panelling. There are two sections of

The Chancel  **The Minister's Manse**

pews, with ample legroom, facing east towards the polygonal shaped, carved pulpit. The beautiful chancel is reached through a Norman style arch with scalloped capitals before reaching the communion table and five wonderfully carved chairs with an ancient bell sitting in front of the table. The north aisle contains a small gallery under a round arch and fronted by an arcaded timber

~ *Cranshaws* ~

screen and lit by another rose window sited on the north wall. The minister's Manse is situated a little north in the same valley as the kirk.

Little Cranshaws could boast the brothers Bertram who invented a contraption for the making of steel rings for cart wheels which greatly reduced time and fuel in the making. They sold their design and the first known instance of it being used elsewhere was at Innerwick in East Lothian before spanning the kingdom. Those brothers, ancestors and descendants, worked the old smiddy for several decades, if not centuries and, for the most part, be busy on what was once a busy thorughfare. The Smiddy, to the north of the hamlet near St. Agnes and Harehead near the Whiteadder at the foot of Duncan Brae.

Though there was never many facilities at Cranshaws in terms of shops, though a grocer is mentioned during the 19th century, a butcher and fishmonger called on a regular basis. Apart from the school, the church and soon to be, village hall, the people were able to borrow a book from their very own local library but, sadly, that is consigned to history, as has the local school, though the building still exists, forcing the children to travel further afield for their education leaving the church and village hall as the principal focal points in the area.

The Rev. J.H. Sibbald commented in 1834 that the parish would never really flourish until there was a better through road on what was once one of the busiest routes through the Borders, what did he know then that is not known now? There is the case, of course, the local people prefer it as it is since new roads attract more traffic and traffic would only help to remove what Cranshaws has to offer, total peace and tranquility. That doesn't mean there is nothing going on, this is a progressive community and the area has so much outdoor activities on offer including the Guild and kids groups. Still, beautiful walks and fishing the Whiteadder can provide endless enjoyment for casual visitors, holiday makers and locals alike. It is always worth checking the local news by way of the Lammermuir Life website to keep up to date with what is going on. One thing which is going on, and it has done for the last five years, but last year, 2015, Audio Soup Music Festival moved to a green field site on the lands of Harehead at Cranshaws.

Audio Soup provide several stages backing up the main stage where many genres of modern music is blasted out to a starry eyed audience while bars and cafés provide all required for an enjoyable gig. Safe, flat camping sites are available as are toilets, ensuring the revellers enjoy not only a fun weekend but also a comfortable one. The 2016 event returns to the Cranshaws venue in July for a fun weekend for all set in the most beautiful setting at the foot of Blackford Rig and Dog Law on the banks of the Whiteadder Water just to the north of the ancient settlement where the cranes dovetailed below the trees as they skimmed the river on their never ending search for food..and now, music.

~ *Edrom with Blanerne* ~

*E*drom is much better known as a parish, than it is a village and, it has to be said, in early times a very important parish indeed. It is bordered by an astonishing ten other parishes and sits right at the heart of mid-eastern Berwickshire. Edrom itself is such a small unassuming hamlet, so few houses, so few people but while never large, it wasn't always that way. In days of old, there was some industry, including a little paper making, linen manufacture, weaving, bleachfields and other cottage industries like sewing and clothes manufacture, There was also at least one shop and a form of local postal service and of course, the eternal agriculture, the farms, Edrom Newton and Mid Edrom still sit on the doorstep. Local people nourished themselves on the fruits of the land and fresh trout from the Whiteadder, the river from which the village took it's original name, 'Ederham' meaning village on the Eder, Ether or Adder, the same word in different languages, all meaning river or water. In later times, it even had its very own rail station on the Berwickshire Line at the foot of the Kelloe Road. So the village on the river, while never climbing the heights of a large town, did achieve greatly in the ecclesiastical world becoming a Rectory and headquarters of a sprawling parish. Edrom Church was also Mother Church to no less than four chapels, East Nisbet (Allanbank) Kimmerghame, Blackadder and the distant chapel at Ercildune (Earlston) some miles to the west.

*O*f course, we have already discussed, the Nisbets, Blackadder and Kimmergehame but another important house and estate of yesteryear was Kelloe House, home of the notable Buchan family, latterly Fordyce-Buchan, but, sadly the main house at Kelloe was demolished in the 1970s. Nearby, on left bank of the Whiteadder, another great house, Blanerne Castle, was home to the notable Lumsdaine family and though now a ruin, it has been replaced by the impressive Blanerne House.

*B*y the 19th century, Edrom was growing smaller as people left in search of work, though the church and school were still busy but those apart, by the middle of that century, Edrom had basically, what we now see. Some lovely houses including the impressive manse, nearby Edrom House which is now used for educational purposes,

The Edrom Arch

137

~ *Edrom* ~

some wonderful farm cottages, an impressively converted steading and the magnificent farm house of Edrom Newton. There is also the old school which was also used a sewing school, now acting as the village hall, and of course, there is the beautiful old church.

*E*legant Edrom, is one of the most beautiful churches, inside and out, in the Scottish Borders. The near cruciform building was built in 1732 retaining what is now the south transcept, built in 1499, containing the Blackadder burial aisle which was founded by Robert Blackadder, Archbishop of Glasgow but later 'taken over' by the new lairds of Blackadder, the Home family. Major refurbishment took place in 1886 but like most churches, renovation, repair and renewal was never ending. Indeed, many episodes of renovation work have been noted over the years, especially in the 14th century when several mentions are made including, in 1332, when the chancel roof was topped with new thatching and special timber, imported from Estland. (Estonia), fitted to hold the thatch.

*P*erhaps, the greatest attraction of all at the atmospheric kirk, is a relic from the original church, a Romanesque arch which was saved when the old kirk was finally demolished in 1737. The wonderful arch with so much intricate detail is now in the care of Historic Scotland and forms the entrance to the burial aisle of the locally prominent Logan family, generous benefactors of the church. The most unusual part of the doorway, apart from the delightful arch and all the detail, are the three steps down then two steps up to enter the aisle allowing visitors to see the full beauty of the medieval work from a slightly lower viewpoint. The earthen floor within the old building reminds us of the floors in nearly every church of the early days.

*T*he origins of the church may lie in the late 11th century when King Edgar granted the lands of Ederham to Gospatric II of Dunbar. Gospatric granted his church, dedicated to the Virgin Mary, and all its tithes, to the monks of Coldingham before his death in 1138, a grant which was confirmed the following year by King David I. There is another version of the origins suggesting the church was in the hands,of an English knight, Thor Longus but that is erroneous since Thor Longus was more associated with the church at Ednam. Ednaham and Ederham (Ednam and Edrom) can easily be confused.

*I*t is important to note, the continuing support of the Scottish royals, during medieval times was paramount to the growth of Christianity in the early development of Scotland. Without that support, the church's growth may have taken a little longer.

*W*illiam de Chattan, Vicaire de l'Eglise de Ederham, (the vicar of the church of Edrom) swore fealty to Edward in 1296 on behalf of the parish and rectory. We also know of Robert of Edrom, a local laird, who gifted lands at Old Cambus to Coldingham around 1203 when he also paid homage to Arnold the Prior and one, Walter Lindsay: Robert later confirmed the same lands to the

~ *Edrom* ~

Priory in 1207.

The magnificent interior of today's church is a more than suitable place for all occasions and it's not surprising the church is so popular with couples wishing a church wedding in the most tasteful and dignified surroundings. Entering from the vestibule to the north of the building there is a central aisle between two sections of pews. In front of those pews is a wider section facing the pulpit on the brightly lit south wall meaning two aisles now split the pews with more seating facing from the east and west. The communion table holds the middle ground in the raised chancel area with steps to the east and west reaching for the pulpit and three communion chairs. A white sandstone baptismal font is situated near the communion table, slightly off centre.

Two great panels depicting the Apostles Creed, the Ten Commandments and the Lord's Prayer adorn the south wall to the east of the pulpit while a great arched, panelled window, behind a lower, timber traceried screen, blocks off the south trancept to the west of the pulpit, and showers light above the Blackadder Burial Vault which, as intimated, was part of the pre-Reformation church. The stained pine pews are surrounded by dado panelling at the lower part of a cream-coloured plastered wall and a simply awesome opened vaulted timber roof. The loft, held by cast iron pillars, above the entrance at the north transcept, is dominated by a great pipe organ which was presented to the church in memory of Lady Euphemia Houston Boswall by her daughter Evelyn. On the carved screen to the front of the gallery is a clock, perhaps reminding the minister that his time is drawing to a close.

While the building itself is of cruciform shape, the interior is laid out in the form of a 'T'. The bright and cheery church, with God's own light flooding through eight windows is supplemented by elaborate carved wood light fittings in the style of the Star of David and hanging from the beamed ceiling. It is a scene set by angels and a visit to this church is a must.

The churchyard is well cared for and exudes a sense of peace, a place where the outside world seems a million miles away. There is an old building near the entrance which is now used as a shed but was probably built as a mort house or even a watch house where bereaved families would maintain a week long vigil, keeping watch for body snatchers. In 1826 there was an incident of body-snatching which resulted in a riot breaking out in Duns. Most body-snatching was carried out to sell the bodies for medical science but even in those days, it very much disgusted the populace, who took action where and when they could. Happily that form of assisting medical science is consigned to the past.

Two of the most important mainstays of the Reformation, the parish church and school, were available to the common people and children, no matter their circumstances or where in Scotland they lived, meaning worship and free education were all within reasonable walking distance from their

~ *Edrom* ~

homes. In the modern day, so many churches are closing or being linked with others, sharing services and far too many schools are closing, meaning bus trips for the children every morning to attend the nearest school. I sometimes wonder if, in the present, more affluent times in which we live, we have lost some of our values and roots.

Edrom Parish Church

from the south-east

*P*erhaps the principal family of the parish were the Blackadders, a name which lives long and sure in the annals of the Borders, Church and Scottish history. Their castle and great house have gone but the family name will live forever. Interestingly, the church at Edrom recently received gifts, from a Blackadder descendent, of their 'universal' family bible from the 18th century accompanied by a book of extensive commentary on the text. The earliest recorded name on the priceless books is dated 1769. Other notables were the Logans, descendants of the Logans of Restalrig in Edinburgh, one of whom, Sir John, accompanied James Douglas in taking the Bruce's heart to the Holy Land. The Logan Home family were the lords at Broom House. Others with association were the ancient family of Swinton, the Fordyce Buchans of Kelloe as we have seen and the Houston Boswalls. The Kelloe family are buried below the north section of today's church. Robert Fortune, the world famous horticulturist, was born in the Parish in 1813 and was educated at the local school before moving on to his fulfil a ground breaking career.

*T*o the west of the churchyard there is a fine arched gateway leading to pasture lands adjacent to Edrom House, for long a home of the Braimer or Bremner family and more recently the home of model, Stella Tennant, grandaughter of the Duke and Duchess of Devonshire but, as we have already seen, is now used for educational and occupational studies.

*T*he churchyard contains many fine stones where many of the local gentry and farmers lie side by side with the more humble among us. There are clear views of the hamlet to the south and the pasture lands to the north and west but

~ *Edrom – Blanerne* ~

the peace and tranquility of Edrom, is, and always will be, all around us.

Edrom Rail Station
Track bed, platform and the ticket office with engine shed in the background

~ *Blanerne* ~

*A*cross the river, a little to the north-east of Edrom, sits the ancient community of Blanerne where existed another of those castles destroyed by Hertford's hoodlums during the Rough Wooing War of the mid 1540s. On our way towards the fine old Todheugh Bridge across the Whiteadder, we pass another of those wonderfully well kept farms, Todheugh, which can be found all over the Borders.

*B*lanerne Castle was, for countless centuries, the home of the locally prominent family of Lumsdaine who were, over the years, considered a caring and benevolent family and trusted lairds of the manor. When the English attacked in 1545, they put up a determined fight but sadly, were no match for the larger, superior forces of the Earl of Hertford. When the troubles were finally over, the family set about re-building their castle, the ruins of which we now see.

*T*he present house at beautiful Blanerne, is now a very fine Bed and Breakfast establishment and is ideally situated in the Whiteadder valley overlooking the invigorating river. Adjacent to Blanerne is the most impressive walled garden and another lovely home, Nelson House and, while there may be, but a few houses left at Blanerne in the modern day, they really are of the highest standard in quality and beauty.

~ *Blanerne – Fogo* ~

The ruins of 16th century, Blanerne Castle overlooking the Whiteadder Water
Courtesy of Walter Baxter

~ *Fogo* ~

The tiny hamlet of Fogo lies just two and a half miles south of Gavinton, across a bridge of 1641 over the Blackadder, a bridge which was built by James Cockburn of Ryeslaw in honour of his parents, James and Margaret. Fogo is but a small community with very few buildings, all huddled along one street joined by Fogo Mains, a little to the east and Caldra House and Farm situated across the river. Fogo, is situated near Chesters where lay a Roman fort, one of the many ancient sites in Berwickshire.

At one time, from the 17th to the 19th centuries, Fogo was a little larger than it is today and could boast two grocer's shops and, it is said, an inn, used mainly for travellers but that is not to say the local people never used it. Having said that, it is said, the population of the parish has never been more than 600 souls but is so much smaller in the present day. Yet in those bygone days, the population supported the local school and the fine church at the bottom of the green. However, what Fogo lacks in size, is more than made up for in history, more particularly of their old church, certainly one of the oldest in Berwickshire, and one of the very few old style buildings still being used in Scotland.

It is not certain when the original church was built but the sign at the kirk gates proudly proclaims the church is from the 11th century though the first mention of the church arrives in 1151 when Gamel is mentioned as the dean of Foghaw. He was chaplain from 1151 until 1160 then again from 1161 until

~ *Fogo* ~

1162. In 1155, the pope, Adrian IV wrote to Abbot Arnold of Kelso informing him that every church in the care of Kelso, including Fogo, should all enjoy the safety and support of the abbot and the benefits of St. Andrews Cathedral. All that tends to do, is confirm the old church was founded during the reign of King David I, if not before.

*M*any grants were made to the abbey over the years by the Cospatrics of Dunbar and their descendants, the Corbett family. In 1172, a man, described simply as J of Fogo confirmed a grant of Haliburton made by his ancestors in earlier times. Other clergymen we know of during medieval times were, John the parson in 1153 who assisted Gamel the dean and another John who was dean at the end of the 12th century. Sir Patrick Corbet was a rector of the church in the latter part of the 13th century while Richard was Rector of Fogo and Linton between 1289 and 1295; William of Fogo was abbot at Kelso from 1310 until 1314 while, earlier, David the vicar of Foghaw, swore fealty to Edward I at Berwick in 1296.

*M*any lords of Fogo, or their sons, granted so much lands over the years, not only to Kelso but also to Melrose Abbey which, from time to time, caused some bitterness between the two abbeys. One of those arguments led to a bitter dispute when William, son of Patrick I of Dunbar, gifted lands to Melrose in 1268, which his son, Nicholas Corbett of Fogo decided

Fogo Kirk – Courtesy of James T M Towill Geograph

to take back, with the permission of the abbot of Melrose, Adam of Paxton, and grant them to the church of Fogo. Some years later, their was a commission assembled to investigate the transactions to which the rector of Fogo, Sir Patrick Corbett, was invited to participate. The result was, Fogo could keep the lands but were ordered to pay, what was described as a 'pittance', to Melrose Abbey, on the feast day of the *Discovery of the 11,000 Virgins* (see over)*

~ *Fogo* ~

The Feast of the Discovery of the 11,000 Virgins stems from Ursulla, a princess in ancient Britain, probably West Wales, who set sail, sometime in the 4th century, to meet her husband to be, Conan Meriadoc of Amorica, thought to be a region of Ancient Germany. Ursulla took with her, 11,000 hand maidens (all virgin girls) but during her trip, she decided to make a pilgrimage to Rome. On her return from Rome, she encountered an army of Huns laying seige to Cologne where she was captured and murdered while her 11,000 maidens were all beheaded. In later times, the body of Ursulla and her followers were discovered and taken to the Basillica of St. Ursulla in Cologne and laid to rest where they are said to remain. In fact bones from the dead have been used to create the walls of the Golden Chamber within the church

Another holy establishment, a priory, dedicated to St. Nicholas, existed at Fogo which was said to be sited on the opposite side of the river and to the west, near Sisterpath. The illustrious Dunbar family granted both houses to Kelso Abbey but it would appear the chapel across the river was more of an early style collegiate church, populated by monks of Kelso Abbey serving only the lordly family and we are indeed fortunate to have the names of two monks and two priors who served the chapel across the water; the monks were, John, in the 12th century and Adam who served in the following century; the priors we know of, were William Leischman during the 15th century and Andrew Graham nearly a century later

Both establishments were consecrated by David de Bernham of St. Andrews but strangely, at different times. The kirk was dedicated in 1243 nearly a year after the chapel which seems strange, making two trips from St. Andrews to dedicate two houses of God separated only by the width of a river. De Bernham was a Borderer, born at Berwick, who served as Chancellor to the King, Alexander II, before becoming bishop. Upon his death in 1253, he was buried at the old kirkyard at Nenthorn.

Today's church at Fogo is probably more akin to the type of church which John Knox would have been very proud of, it is so plain and still retains its box pews and the precentor's desk and chair in front of the pulpit. It is a place, Knox may have had cause to celebrate at the local inn with the Precentor of the kirk, joining the great man and the Kirk Minister to toast the well being of the beautiful old church and school.

The kirk contains two lofts, one on the east and the other on the west which were the domains of the local lairds, the Hog family of Harcarse and the Trotters of Charterhall. The Trotters donated the Communion Cups in 1683 and they now play a leading roll in the church. The congregation of Fogo still promote the The Tradition of the *"Priesthood of Believers"* using the ancient cups and a common loaf. Both the Bread and the Wine are passed from person to person around the kirk, linking each person not only with others in the kirk

~ *Fogo* ~

on the same day, but also with many worshippers throughout the centuries.

An ancient headstone, possibly as old as the 14th century, is contained in the old vestry while so many fine stones are to be found in the kirkyard including the stone cast on the south wall, of three figures with the sentiment, *Vive Memor Lethi* - 'Live remembering Lethi' – the river of the afterworld. There are also 15 gravestones to the men who died at nearby RAF Charterhall during the Second World War. Another interesting grave stone is the one dedicated to Yorkie, the tramp who often spent time at Fogo. At the entrance to the kirkyard, stands the most atmospheric Lychgate and Parish War Memorial, a sobering sight when going to church.

I have got to confess, Fogo is one of my favourite churches. Looking over the old village green, seeing this wonderful old building, parts of which must up to 1,000 years old, make me tremble with pride, it is the kind of kirk I have always perceived a Scottish church should be. It is so plain and yet it is the very plainness of the building which appeals. If what is said, 'beauty is in the eyes of the beholder' is true, then I am the beholder of the beauty that is Fogo Parish Church.

The former school at Fogo, now the nursery

*I*n earlier times, the parish boasted, apart from the everlasting agriculture, several quarries, corn mills, barley mills, brewery and cooperage, a tile works, two grocers, as mentioned, a tailor and a railway station to the west at Marchmont. Add that to a thriving little church and a well attended school and you'd be forgiven for thinking Fogo was a larger, more populated place but it was and is, at best, small. It was reported in 1834, the parish as a whole consisted of just over 500 souls of which, only 35 resided in the hamlet. It is interesting to note, the population of the hamlet of Fogo had reduced to only 21 in 2004. While many agricultural trades remain servicing the surrounding farms, and farming itself, the tailor, grocers and all the other works have long

~ *Fogo* ~

since departed the scene. The village school too has closed but is now being used as a very popular nursery, so to a degree, the children are still receiving some early education.

The railway station at nearby Marchmont was of great benefit before the coming of the motor car, to locals who had plans to travel, visiting other communities or further afield but moving around locally was a little more difficult if you didn't own a horse. In time, everyone owned a bicycle which took them from A to B but, in reality, the roads were never meant for anything else, they were so quiet, but that all changed during the Second World War when RAF Charterhall opened.

Old RAF building at Charterhall

The War Department requisitioned a great swathe of Charterhall and converted it to an air base complete with a large runway and all the buildings required of an important military base. Many locals would, of course be employed on the site helping to take care of the station's every need. Sadly many men of RAF Charterhall died during the conflict and evidence of that can be seen at the Commonwealth Graves in Fogo Kirkyard and the nearby memorial to Battle of Britain ace, Richard Hillary and his radio man Wilfrid Fison who perished on a training flight from Charterhall in January 1943. The runway at Charterhall was then used for motor racing from 1952 until 1964 but is now a private air strip.

The family who own the great estate and magnificent house, are the notable Trotters of Mortonhall and Charterhall. It is a family who have been most benevolent to Fogo and the region in general over the years and so many have served with distinction, indeed two men from that family are depicted on Fogo's stunning War Memorial, Lt-Col. Edward H. Trotter of the Grenadier Guards and Capt. Reginald B. Trotter of the Cameron Highlanders. In the year 2000, Major Alexander Richard Trotter of Mortonhall and the 5th of Charterhall, the chief of the name and arms of the Clan Trotter, was appointed Her Majesty's Lord Lieutenant for Berwickshire, a post he served faithfully until 2014. Another notable family in the area is the Milne-Homes, a cadet family of the Homes of Wedderburn and who own the magnificent Caldra House. Caldra, castle and original house was built by the Cockburns of Langton and they remained in possession until Charles Cockburn, son of Sir

~ *Fogo* ~

Charles sold the property to Dr. Patrick Home of Wedderburn in 1745. Charles had only ascended to the property three years earlier on the death of his older brother, William.

Today, there is no air base nor railway station, the quarries are redundant and the wheels of the watermills, on the eternal Blackadder, no longer turn. Agriculture, for various reasons, is not so busy and the church is only open once a month month for service. It can be visited any time though, during daylight hours, and, should you visit, you will not be disappointed. The minister at Fogo is the long serving Reverend Alan Cartwright (for more details, see Swinton)

While you are there, take a walk down the path adjacent to the kirkyard, until you reach the River Blackadder where you will arrive at the old ford, now crossed by the John Hunter Bridge **(above)** erected in 2004 in memory of Rev. John Hunter who was minister of the church from 1926 until 1965. On the subject of John Hunter, a lady, who was so instrumental in having the wonderful bridge built in his honour, Lisa Chernoff, was given the proud honour of planting 'The Fogo Tree' on the green near the church commemorating the Queen's Diamond Jubilee of her ascension to the throne in 1952 but the children from Fogo Nursery School were not about to be undone, they planted a commemorative tree too.

Fogo is a bonnie place and though small, contains some fine houses from social housing to old farm cottages and other larger homes including the old manse. The small green to the south of the church and the surrounding trees do add a splash of colour to the peaceful scene. There are excellent walks all around including along the riverside, so far removed from the business of the larger towns. So sweet and gentle is this area of Fogo, it really is set in its very own 'Garden of Eden'

~ *Gavinton* ~

Gavinton, just two miles south-west of Duns, is a lovely village, planned and laid out to the south of the old Langton Estate, complete with a large green, by David Gavin and his wife Lady Elizabeth Maitland, daughter of the 7th Earl of Lauderdale soon after they purchased the Langton Estate, in 1758, from the eminent Cockburn family of Berwickshire. Gavin's reasoning behind the building of the new village in his name was, he was, frankly, getting frustrated with the village and villagers of Langton living in his 'back garden'. Moving villagers out of estates, building a new village then destroying the old was something which was being carried out all over Scotland during the 18th and 19th centuries. While the village and its people had been removed, the old Kirk of Langton remained on the estate for some years to follow.

Ancient Langton has a long and distinguished history though, at the end, a tinge of sadness. The de Ow (or d'Eu) family built the first Langton Castle in the form of a tower and as we shall see, it was they who granted the original kirk of Langton to Kelso. The de Ow family did not appear to settle too long before the distinguished family of de Veteriponte (Vipont) family took over and it was almost certain certainly that family who built a small chapel on the estate a little to the west of the castle. During their reign, Langton experienced many changes, there was much renewal and expansion on the lands and industry was introduced, including several quarries. Many cot houses were built to house the estate workers and, for the time being, all was well on one of the great estates of Berwickshire. That is until tragedy struck on the 24th June, 1314 when Sir William de Vipont was killed fighting the good cause on the fields of Bannockburn. Slightly later, William's daughter Mariota (or Mary) married Sir William Cockburn thus carrying the lands of Langton to that family who then proceeded to enlarge and 'modernise' the castle. That particular family drove industry forward and during their tenure of some centuries, spinning and weaving was introduced just as it was on their other lands in Haddingtonshire.

In 1496, the Cockburn family 'welcomed' the king, James IV who arrived on the scene and stationed his artillery on the estate in preparation for an attack in to England. The king then rode to Ellem to meet the rest of his army but no attack materialised. That particular king had threatened to attack the north of England several times and though his stay at Langton was extended, no invasion was undertaken. However, some 17 years later, the king did attack, with much success, a success which lead to the errors and tragedy of Flodden in 1513. In 1565, that king's grand daughter, Mary of Scots spent a night at Langton during an inspection of the border lands.

The Cockburns were one of Scotland's wealthiest families and possessed much lands throughout south-east Scotland, particularly Berwickshire and East Lothian. They would become the Barons of Duns and were the builders of two other castles in the neighbourhood, one at nearby Borthwick and the other

~ *Gavinton* ~

north of Duns. However all was not as it seemed, rich people were often the victims of attack and that scenario arrived at Langton in 1558, when the entire village, church, chapel and tower were attacked by Sir Henry Percy, earl of Northumberland whose forces caused so much damage and destruction to every building on the estate. It took more than a century to finally reinstate all the buildings on the estate and surrounding farms.

When Sir Alexander Cockburn of Langton died at the Battle of Fontenoy in 1745, another chapter in the parish was coming to an end. As we have read, the Gavins took over in 1758 and wasted no time in demolishing all in sight before building a new mansion-house, but it was their descendants, the Breadalbanes, who, in the latter part of the 19th century, demolished the house and built one of the most magnificent houses ever to be rooted on Scottish soil, Langton House (see Great Houses) The estates later passed to Elizabeth, Lady Pringle then finally to her daughter, Mary Gavin-Pringle who later married Robert Baillie-Hamilton, son of the 10th Earl of Haddington and it was that couple, who built the last, and most magnificent Langton House. In 1920, the family left Langton forever before, in 1940, the estate and house were used by a Polish detachment who were serving on the side of the allies in the Second World War. Sadly the once proud home of the descendants of David Gavin, was demolished in 1950.

Old Langton Church, which had been dedicated in the name of St. Cuthbert on 6th April, 1242 by David de Bernham of St. Andrews, stayed on the estate for a while but so many repairs over the years meant its days were always being 'counted'.

As early as 1684, during the Episcopacy, Langton Church of the 11th/12th century, was reported as having required no repairs, which seems a strange situation for a building of such antiquity, this lends to the theory that the church, inspected at that time, was probably at least, the second church on the site and there is some evidence of a new church being built after the English Wardens' attack of 1558. That inspection of 1684, was carried out on behalf of the Bishop of Edinburgh during the ministry of Patrick Walker. Further visitations were made in 1700 when the church desperately required attention and in 1717 when the roof was ruinous before finally collapsing in 1721. More major repairs were carried out allowing the poor old building to survive until 1798 when a new church was built in the new village.

Because of Langton Kirk's antiquity and prominence, we are indebted to have been furnished with so many of the men who bore connection with the parish. A man known simply as Henry was the first known parson when he was mentioned in 1152 while other early parsons we know of are, Herbert at the turn of the 12th century and John who had the 'distinction' of swearing fealty to Edward of England in 1296 at Berwick along with Peronal de Vipont of Langton. They followed in the footsteps of Allanus of Langetoun who swore

~ *Gavinton* ~

allegiance to the same king in 1291. In the later part of the 14th century, the church was without a priest and the heritor, Richard Cockburn was released of his post in favour of 18 year old, Andrew de Balmentacal though that situation was short lived. As we know David de Bernham dedicated the church while others who joined de Bernham at the ceremony included John of Kelso and Hugh, Abbot of Kelso. Others of whom we know of included Walter, a local feu holder, Nicholas who was a burgess at Berwick and Patrick, Ralph and Robert, all designated 'of Langton' and who all witnessed many charters of the 12th and 13th centuries, as did John, again 'of Langetoun'.

The church of 1798 was replaced in 1872, on the instructions of Lady Elizabeth Pringle, and was designed and built by James Maitland Wardop one of the 19th century's most prominent architects who also designed Ayton Church in Berwickshire. It is built in a First Pointed, Gothic style with a four-bay rectangular nave and a four-stage square tower corniced at the top with a pinnacled finial at each corner and pointed bay air vents on each side. The tower is topped by a two-stage octagonal spire, reaching for the sky, with a weathercock on top. In more recent times, some local boys, playing with air guns, are said to have shot holes in the poor old cockerel but it has since been repaired. The south wall is of a masoned local sandstone while the other walls are of rubblestone.

It is a magnificent church inside and out and a worthy successor to a truly ancient church. The interior contains many memorials including one gifted by a Polish soldier and dedicated to his late wife, Isabella Borzestoska. An organ which was gifted to the church by the wife and family of Reverend James Longmuir CBE, TD, DD and dedicated to that great man, a former minister at the kirk and a Moderator of the General Assembly of the Church of Scotland. There is also a plaque presented to the church by HMS Gavinton, a minesweeper of the Royal Navy.

Langton Parish Church

Many fine memorials adorn the walls and a large collection of old communion tokens from Langton Kirk and Langton Free Church, are on

~ *Gavinton* ~

display, as is a complete list of ministers of Langton. On the adjacent window ledge sits the old parish 'deid bell' which would be rung outside a deceased person's home then used to lead the cortege to the funeral. That bell is not used in the modern day and neither is the bell in the tower. The church still possesses photographs of its founder, Lady Pringle and two volumes of bibles gifted by Mary Gavin.

The parish kirk was affected badly at the time of the Disruption in 1843 when the minister of the day, Rev. John Brown and most of the congregation walked out to form their own Free Kirk which, initially was held in a barn on the Langton Estate. Soon though, they built their own church, a building which still stands as a private residence, near the junction with the Duns to Greenlaw road. Rev. Brown, of course, was the first minister at the new kirk while the last was Thomas Anderson before the congregation and church reunited with the parish church in 1929. Langton Parish Church is part of Langton and Lammermuir Church. Mrs. Helen Longmuir, the former Session Clerk and wife of the previously mentioned, late minister and moderator, the Reverend James, died recently and I know, from personal experience as with so many others, Helen Longmuir will be very, very sadly missed, she was a wonderful lady with a spirit of giving, to us all.

Gavinton Village Hall incorporating the old village school and the Butterwell Hall

Today's Gavinton is a bonnie place, drive through at your peril, you'd miss so much of the charm of the model village. Many fine houses are situated on the Main Street which also boasted the original school and schoolhouse on opposite sides of the road. There was too, for many years in Gavinton, a very popular inn. Many atmospheric cottages on Maitland and South Streets with a huddle of fine houses and cottages around the village green which, originally, was meant to be a market square. At the south east corner of the green stands the village hall, where all the local clubs including the Women's Rural, coffee mornings and other activities take place. The hall was greatly improved in 2008 and contains rooms and halls for all occasions. There is also a community cinema based in the hall and regular showings are always well

~ *Gavinton* ~

attended. The village hall is based in an old building which once served as the school and is now co-joined with the Butterwell Hall. Why Butterwell? you may ask; it is named after an old Butter Well which is situated only a few yards down on the road to Fogo and once served, I am told, as the cooling place for locally produced butter, which was said to have been made in abundance in the village. To the east of the village hall, in South Street, where another old 'drawing' well still stands. Further to the east, many other fine private houses have been built on Main Street while The Glebe has, in more recent times, been tastefully built over by a social housing estate further increasing the size of the bonnie village.

*I*n June, 2009, the villagers, dressed in 18th century style clothing, gathered to make a nostalgic visit to Old Langton to mark the 250th anniversary of the founding of the new village. They assembled at the ruins of the old kirk and the graveyard where many of the stones were found to be in excellent condition with the earliest dated 1620 (the oldest known, still standing, in the Scottish Borders} right up to the last burial in 1859.

*O*ne last look around the church compound, sitting at the highest point in the village where wonderful views are to be had of the surrounding countryside. My thoughts turned to the church hall and the condition of the wonderful church, all the residue of a hard working Kirk Session and congregation as a whole. We sometimes forget the work and thought that goes in to the smooth running of a church and what I saw at Langton is indicative of nearly every parish in the Borders of Scotland.

*T*hough there are no longer shops nor business in the village, but at one time, and not in the too distant past, Gavinton was blessed with many shops including grocers, a baker and services like the post office, joiners, blacksmith, stonemason, an inn and, of course, a fine wee school, allowing the children to be educated locally. The most renowned of all the business people were the Lillies of Langton, who were the local blacksmiths for generations before and after the great shift, from old Langton to new Gavinton. The main source of income in those times was farming, milling, with the most enduring being Langton Mill and some quarrying operations. While nothing of the above exists in the present day there is a steel fabrication company nearby.

*I*t is of course, no coincidence, since the introduction of supermarkets in towns, shops in villages have gone by the wayside. What I believe to be more sad, is the loss of the post office and school but unfortunately, money takes precedence over services and very few small villages like Gavinton have their own post offices in the society in which we now live. The greatest of all dreams of the reformed Scottish Kirk, a school in every parish has long since gone by the wayside as we have seen elsewhere, including Gavinton School, even though more houses have been built in the present day and more will be built in the future, the school has almost certainly, gone forever.

~ *Gavinton - Greenlaw* ~

Perhaps the biggest day in Gavinton's Calendar is the visit of the Duns Reiver and his entourage during the Duns Summer Festival. All gather at the village hall in anticipation of the arrival of the great cavalcade.

Before leaving the village, let us look at a small obelisk memorial (**right, courtesy of James Allan - Geograph**) to Ann Smith, an Irish lady who gave Lady Elizabeth Pringle forty years of unstinting and faithful service for which the good lady erected this monument in her friend's honour, a lovely touch from wonderful and much loved lady of the manor. That monument helps sum up the benevolence of Lady Pringle, who did so much for the people of Gavinton. The memorial is situated near the house which now occupies the old Free Kirk and opposite the large, well used, sports fields, another valuable facility in the region.

~ *Greenlaw* ~

The old County Town of Berwickshire, Greenlaw, is situated some seven miles south-west of Duns, the town with which Greenlaw vied for centuries for the county honours. It sits in the vale of the eternal Blackadder Water which nonchalantly flows through on her eternal journey towards her sister river, the Whiteadder. The Berwickshire railway once connected the town with the outside world but in 1948 was violently swept away during rain storms causing the river to sweep aside everything in its way. The town centre, shops and homes took a battering from the Blackadder, an event they had never experienced before...nor since. The people of the ancient Burgh of Barony soon recovered, got on with their lives, but sadly without their beloved rail link which was never re-opened.

Greenlaw, it seems, followed a similar path to Duns almost to the letter. Early inhabitation by hill dwellers, a 'visit' from the Romans and further attacks and domination from the Angles, Saxons, Danes, Northumbrians and the English all mixed with the more friendly faces of the early Apostles of Lindisfarne offering some solace to the hard pressed people of the Green Law, around a mile south of the present town. So many finds over the years, both

~ *Greenlaw* ~

north, at Blackcastle Rings and Heriots Dyke, and south of the town at Chesters, quite clearly shows there was much early habitation while even more digs produced evidence of Roman and early Anglo-Saxon activity. Edward I 'visited' the area as did Edward III during his *Burnt Candlemas* sorties and there is absolutely no doubt, the old church was destroyed by those devils. Hertford was another who ravaged the town, church and castle during Henry VIII's *Rough Wooing* of the Scottish Court but, by that time, the town and people had long since moved from the eminence of the Law to the flatter lands above the Merse meaning their move came much earlier than their neighbours to the east. Greenlaw became the county seat for Berwickshire in the 15th century when Berwick was, more or less, annexed by the English.

There is legend, with foundation, of an old burial place to the east of Old Greenlaw which has led historians of yesteryear to believe a church existed from as early as the 7th century. Christianity was spreading northwards in to south-eastern Scotland from Durham and Lindisfarne and Greenlaw may have been be one of the earliest 'recipients' of a place of worship in Berwickshire though many local churches can lay claim to being the first in the region.

The first written evidence of the existence of Greenlaw came in the 11th century when Gospatric of Dunbar was granted the lands by Malcolm III, yet another patch of Berwickshire the powerful Northumbrian family had received since their arrival in Scotland during that century. It is not certain when the first church was erected on the site of the present church but we know of the Dunbars granting that church and the tithes of the mill to the monks of Kelso Abbey in 1147. At that stage, Greenlaw Church had three dependent chapels, at Lambden, Halyburton and Rowiestone which were later confirmed to Kelso by William de Lamerton. Sadly, all three chapels have long since disappeared almost without trace though legend lingers. One legend of old is associated with Rowiestone Chapel, situated just to the north-east of Angelrow Farm. When the chapel, which is thought to have had connection with Eccles Priory, was 'working', the nuns would make their daily procession to their gardens causing local people to describe that sight as a *'Raw of Angels'* or Angels' Row thus the name of the farm. Most names and expressions we now know are derived from local legend and, very often, the legend is in fact, reality, as is probably the case at Angel's Row.

So much is documented of early Greenlaw parish and we know of so many men who lived or worked there including Nigel, a parson who 'doubled' as a lieutenant under Earl Patrick in the mid 12th century while another of note was William de Greenlaw, the master of the town, in a charter of 1180 but they are just two of the many. More men we know from very early times includes Robert of Greenlaw who was Master William's clerk, Roland, probably a burgess, in1208, Matthew of Greenlaw, the Mayor of Berwick who swore fealty to Edward I in 1296 as did Nicholas de Camb, the Vicar of Greenlaw.

~ *Greenlaw* ~

Others included another Matthew of Greenlaw who was a leading Burgess in Kelso and yet another William who was said to be in attendance at Roxburgh during an English attack around the time of the fealty performances at Berwick in 1296. Another eminent with association was David de Bernham, Bishop of St. Andrews and Chancellor of Scotland, who consecrated the church at Greenlaw on 2nd April, 1242 and, though it is not recorded, he would almost certainly dedicate the building to St. Helen as at Aldcambus to the north. Sceptics may say St. Helen has no connection with the burgh but there is a connection which was shown when the king, James VI, created Greenlaw a Burgh of Barony in the dying years of the 16th century mentioning his *Ecclessia de Sancta Helena.*

The Cospatrics held much lands in the area and were thought to have built a tower-house at Whiteside though probably only using it for visits preferring to live at Hume Castle following their assumption of that name. Other proprietors in the parish were the Brounfields (or Broumfield) and the Cranston and Redpath families. The Cranstons didn't last long before, in 1596, they resigned the barony in favour of Sir George Home of Dunbar, High Treasurer of Scotland who almost certainly extended Greenlaw Castle on the right bank of the Blackadder Water near Castle Mill. Another local family of the Hume or Home dynasty, were the Humes of Polwarth later Earls of Marchmont (see Marchmont House)

Greenlaw Castle is thought to have been built in in the 13th century by William de Greenlaw a member of the Dunbar and March family and the first to assume the name of the settlement. He and his wife Ada (his cousin) also owned Hume Castle which had been a gift to Ada from her father, and from that couple, William and Ada, the noble name of Hume (or Home) were descended. Greenlaw Castle passed in to the hands of the de Cranston family who were thought to have received the honour of Greenlaw, as a Burgh of Barony by James II in the early 15th century but it must be emphasised they were granted the status of Barony and not Burgh at that point. The castle then passed through the hands of the Redpaths before returning to the Homes in the shape of Sir George Home the future 1st Earl of Dunbar of the second creation. It was during his reign at Greenlaw, in 1598, the great honour of Burgh of Barony was granted by King James VI, in the name of St. Helen.

Anne Home of Dunbar, Sir George's daughter, and her husband, Sir James Home of Cowdenknowes were the next proprietors of the Barony and castle before it passed to their great nephew, Sir Alexander Home of Manderston. The Castle stayed in that family, until, at least 1730 when it became part of a farm complex and was finally demolished in the mid 19th century. All that remains of the great fort is a mound in the middle of a field.

At the time of George of Dunbar being created Baron, the Kirktoun of Greenlaw was already the main centre of population, the parish town and soon

~ *Greenlaw* ~

a market cross was built, signifying the right to hold markets and fairs, and a common hall (town hall) for carrying out the burgh's business. The Baron was granted those rights and ordered the fairs be held twice yearly, one of which, to be held on the feast day of town's patron saint, St. Helen. The fairs and markets were held round the market cross on the village green, before the days of the new county hall. The shaft of the old cross **(left)** stands at the west gable of the church tower while a new one was erected in the 19th century, now situated behind the Parish War Memorial.

*J*ust over a century later, the county privileges passed to Duns but, when the new baron, Patrick Hume, Lord Polwarth and 1st of Marchmont arrived, he 'put things right' and Greenlaw was restored to what was perceived as its rightful status in 1696. In time, a wonderful county building was erected but all to no avail. Progressively more county responsibility was passed again to Duns before, in 1903, the end had come when Greenlaw's proud title was removed forever. While the importance, industry and population have, to a great degree, diminished, and the railway station closed. The entry signs to the town still proudly proclaims Greenlaw as 'The Ancient County Town of Berwickshire'

*T*o get some idea of how important Greenlaw was, and its ability to attract more people, we just have to take a look at a directory of 1826

The County Hall and War Memorial at Greenlaw
Courtesy of Carol Trotter

156

~ *Greenlaw* ~

to give us some perception to the hustle and bustle of a busy wee town. Have a look at this impressive list of businesses etc. : A Post Office, two baker's shops, ten grocers (five of them selling wines and spirits) four inns including the Castle Inn, eight shoemakers, four blacksmiths, five carpenters, two coopers, several smiths, twelve drapers and dress makers, hand and loom weavers including a large factory and tailors, all making the end products of the farms and the linen and lint mills. Waulk mills, corn and barley mills lining the River Blackadder, providing more employment while other trades included bleach fields and dye houses, the list goes on and on. Another impressive directory of the town of 1881 can be viewed in Carol Trotter's fine article on the Town Hall website. Some of those industries survived for many, many years after World War II in the mid twentieth century.

It was, at that time and beyond, an extremely busy and populous locale and was able to sustain three churches, the Parish, the Free and the United Presbyterian, two doctors, a private school, free church school and the parish school. Add to that, the jailers, surveyors, lawyers, watch makers and the sheriff's Officers. All the trades of the day were busy as was the daily coach between Duns and Edinburgh. Other carriers carried goods to Duns, Coldstream and Edinburgh every day before, during and after the railways came to the town in the second half of the 19th century.

Holy worship was always an important part of the lives of the citizens and, as we have seen, a church was in existence since early times. To this day the parish church still stands proud overlooking the Square, a majestic scene indeed as she overlooks the great and the good of the Parish who lie in the old kirkyard.

In 1675, the pre-Reformation kirk was greatly restored to the point it was a virtual rebuild though some were aggrieved it was not a totally new building, thus totally Protestant. It is noted with interest, there does seem some signs on the exterior walls, since the rough cast was removed some years ago, the church was raised in height and certain markers on the walls appear to confirm that; certainly the church was ultimately added to on the west and is now adjoined to the tolbooth clock tower. During that work, up to three floors were found under the existing building holding, what can best be described as graveyards

The Parish Church

~ *Greenlaw* ~

complete with headstones. Many skeletons were found in the process, buried in an orderly fashion. All that tends to point to another, even earlier church, (from the 12th century?) being built in a different position thus the bodies found were buried in, what was then the graveyard. When the present church had further renovation, more bones were found and the same thing happened twice in the 19th century when heating and drainage systems were being installed. Apart from an earlier rebuild, which I have already described, the only other explanation is, before the Reformation, many of the dead were buried in the church underneath the earthen floors.

The 'church tower' was built in 1712 but was never intended to be for the church, it was a tolbooth (jail) and a courthouse was added to the west to dole out punishments before the convicted were sent 'next door' to 'hell's hole' as the tolbooth became known.

An old rhyme from that time seemed to be written in stone with the words :

"Here stands the gospel and the law
wi' hell's hole atween the twa"

While the clock-tower is now adjoined to the church, there is no passage from one to the other. There was a window from the tower through to the kirk allegedly to allow prisoners to view, or even take part in the

Old County Jail, courtesy of Carol Trotter

service and a mark on the upper wall at the west gallery appears to confirm that. The court house adjoined that tower but was demolished when a new court house in the county hall was opened. Another jail for the whole county was later built near and behind the point where the former bank stands today. It

~ *Greenlaw* ~

was described in 1824, only weeks after it was built, as a more than adequate building - it contained 18 cells for those who would be spending some time 'behind bars', two day rooms where books were made available to those who could read and where they were served their meals. Petty criminals had their own day room but they all shared the exercise yards. The whole compound was surrounded by tall, strong walls. Interestingly the old jail keepers' house still stands as a private home though for many years was used as the police station.

The old church is set in its own kirkyard containing many fine stones, symbolic, table and a 15th century cross slab, while some of the more important members of the community had their own burial plots mapped around the graveyard. On reaching the tower, the first notable structure is the shaft of the original Greenlaw (mercat) Cross, a reminder of the prominent days of yesteryear. The shaft stands alongside the tower which still contains its original, grim iron grill gate and is joined on that wall by a truly ancient head stone.

The church building is of random rubblestone with ashlar dressings and there are no less than nine windows gracing the south elevation, two on the west, one on the east and four on the north. Apart from the great 78 feet tall tolbooth tower there is another tower like structure with a turnpike stairway, added at the east of the main tower. The steeply sloping roof is covered in grey slate and the gables are endowed with period crowsteps. With the addition of the north aisle in 1855, the building was transformed from a rectangle to 'T' shape.

The vestry, on the north, is full of memories, old and new photographs of ministers and Kirk Sessions through the ages grace the walls, and another of HRH Princess Margaret, who attended a service in 1952 while she was staying at Marchmont. Another old frame contains a painting of the old county building with the church, tolbooth and courthouse in the background.

West Gallery at Greenlaw Kirk with the great organ on the right

It is a wonderful building, well worthy of being, at one stage, the church of the most important town and parish in the county of Berwick.

~ *Greenlaw* ~

It still dominates, as it has always done, tall and proud. The minister is the well respected Rev. Thomas Nicholson who has been serving the communities of Berwickshire since 1995. Greenlaw Church is linked with Gordon, linked with Westruther, linked with Legerwood. The first to preach at the church after the Reformation in 1560, was the 'reader', Charles Home, who was almost certainly a priest of the old faith who also held the chaplaincy at Halyburton.

On the 5th April, 2015, no less a day than Easter Sunday, the churches were honoured with the visit of the Moderator of the General Assembly of the Church of Scotland, the Right Reverend John Chalmers at Westruther Kirk.

Another two churches as we have seen, were built in the small town; the United Presbyterian Church, an association of three congregations, opened in the late 18th century on High Street near the Old Castle Inn, first as an anti Burgher Church until 1855 when the UP took it over. Later it was home to a Congregational Church then a garage after its days of holy worship were over. A now demolished Secession/Free Church opened in 1843, the year of the disruption of the church, and was situated on the opposite side of the High Street but a little to the west. That church was later known as the 'Fairbairn' Church, with good cause as we shall see.

It is thought there has been a school in the parish since the 17th century and the present school, the third, still stands on the same piece of land. In the early days, children were taught not only the 3 rs but many also received a form of higher education including Latin and Mathematics. Of course today, only primary school education is taught before all the children move to Berwickshire High School in Duns for their higher or secondary education. For some years following the opening of the Free Church, the minister, Reverend John Fairbairn, a man who was taught at Greenlaw Parish School and Edinburgh University, founded the Free Church School which existed until the re-unification of the churches in the earlier part of the 20th century.

The County or Town Hall and courthouse was the scene of countless court cases over the years and, being the principal court of the region's justiciary, was witness to all forms of crime, from the petty to the especially serious including murder with the powers to condemn the guilty to the ultimate sentence, death. In actual fact, the very last public hanging in Berwickshire took place at Greenlaw Kirk on the 2nd April, 1834 when Mannus Swinney, an Irishman, was executed for assault and robbery.

The hall was built between 1828 and 1831 by Sir William Purves Hume-Campbell, Baronet of Marchmont, in the Greek Revival style. The hall served its purpose as county headquarters and court until 1904 but as we have seen, its days as county headquarters had come and gone. Of course, when the county duties were finally removed to Duns forever, Greenlaw was a much quieter settlement though still busy with travellers on one of the principal routes between north and south. Indeed, the Castle Inn which was almost

- *Greenlaw* -

certainly built around the same time as the County Hall, was still kept busy with those travellers and of course provided for the garaging of the coaches and horses. Perhaps not so grand as housing the many lawyers and judges who attended the local courthouse, but nonetheless, busy. Even during the days of omnibus travel between Edinburgh and London, the Castle was a very popular stopping point.

In later times, the hall was used as a community or village hall where much of the local socialising took place. It was later used to billet Polish soldiers during World War II when it had a near miss when, on April 7th 1941 German planes dropped bombs only yards away destroying a house in the process.

The hall was then used as a swimming pool but for many years it lay unused. In 2006, the hall was shortlisted on the BBC programme, *Restoration Village* but, while the building did not win the competition to be fully restored, it did highlight the dreadful plight of such an iconic structure. Its appearance on the show did ignite the fire of interest and soon gifts of money came flowing resulting in the masterpiece being restored and now, having been wholly refurbished, perhaps there are chinks of light for a brighter future. The building renovations complete, it was reopened by HRH Prince Charles, Duke of Rothesay, in June 2011 to rousing approval, from a large assembly, and now it is a case of finding suitable uses to maintain the building as a viable project like letting space for offices. The regeneration of the beautiful old building, one of the most magnificent in the entire country, could mean a new beginning for the ancient village. Sadly however, it has lain virtually unused but in August 2015, exciting new plans to use the west wing have been announced with the Community Council 'moving in' on a short term lease in an effort to re-ignite interest in the building which will also be made available to members of the public to have access to the internet. The other fine building we looked at, the Castle Inn, is now known as Castletoun House and is a private residence though the owners are willing to let the old stables and garages out to any suitable business venture.

While looking over the village centre, it is easy to see why Greenlaw was such an important place, there is a good solid, permanent feel all around and an air of importance and confidence still exists. That special pride and confidence will always be associated with the old county town, one of the most historic in Scotland and maybe one day soon, the importance will return, hopefully in the form of more industry and jobs to what was once the most important community in the old Berwickshire. Life of course, goes unabated in the old burgh and there is so much going on; while the curlers and their pond have long gone, as has the golf course, there is a well established amateur football team which currently plays in the Border League, Division B, a welcoming bowling club, golf club (though their own course has now closed) yoga classes and a zumba group, fishing club, a branch of the Scottish Women's Institute,

~ *Greenlaw* ~

Church Guild, Equibuddy (riding for the disabled) GR8 club for younger children, art group, first responders, horticultural society, a 'walk it' group, a Masonic Lodge, Horticultural Society and the Greenlaw Festival Trust who take care of and organise the town's annual festival which has grown in popularity year on year over more than fifty years of existence. One of the town's great highlights during the Festival, is the installation of the *Greenlaw Maid* on the last Saturday of June each year. The Maid is usually a first year pupil at Berwickshire High School with her court made up of boys and girls from Greenlaw Primary School. The Greenlaw Maid for 2015 was Samantha Hogg who was crowned by the Lady Lieutenant for Berwickshire, Jeanna Swan who then declared the Festival, open.

Another day on the local calendar was the Greenlaw Games which were at the end of June for many decades. The Games were held in the field which later became known as Happer Park and consisted of races from under-8s (boys and girls) to senior, professional athletes. Everything for a successful, enjoyable day was laid and the park was never less than full. Other old sports and games were carried out 'in the wings' including the popular, ancient game of quoits. Sadly the games died out before 1970.

Quite apart from the grand old County Hall, there are other halls in the town, like the Fairbairn Hall, formerly the Free Church School and the Good Templars Hall of 1892 which changed to the War Memorial Club in 1919 but is now known simply as the War Memorial Hall and is situated in Bank Street. The hall was originally opened for the benefit of the community and following recent refurbishment after some years of decay, the building has been returned to its original principal, and use. That hall contains a coffee shop, Poppy's, Where the staff give of their time freely,

Heading to the Square, courtesy of Carol Trotter

and is open Tuesday to Saturday each week. There is a used book stall, a small museum and, of course, the hall, which is available for all occasions, whether it be social, educational or business and is used by some of the local clubs. There is restaurant and chip shop on East High Street and of course the Blackadder Hotel, not forgetting the facilities at the bowling club.

Greenlaw has a good mix of housing from what may have been old mill

~ *Greenlaw* ~

buildings, cottages, villas, a few flats and larger town houses. There is a nice blend of private and social homes and excellent housing for the senior members of the society. Apart from the main thoroughfares, other enchanting wynds lead off, like Todholes being joined by Mill Wynd while newer streets include Fairbairn Court which was opened by HM Queen Elizabeth in July, 1994, Church Hill, the Avenue and Blackadder Crescent.. More fine houses can be found on the Edinburgh Road, Marchmont Road and Wester Row.

If ever proof was needed of this being one of the principal meeting points in the Borderlands, you have it here where six roads lead in to town from every point of the compass. The roads lead from Earlston and Gordon, from Coldstream, from Edinburgh and Lauder, the moors road from Duns, the minor road from Halyburton and finally, Marchmont Road from where you can reach Marchmont House passing some, perceived to be, ancient earthworks and the site of a Roman fort at Chesters. Many farms are situated along every route and all use the wee town for everyday shopping and social relaxation.

Apart from what has already been mentioned, today's wee burgh contains two shops, one of them, the former Post Office, two inns, a butcher's shop, two garage businesses, an internet café, the New Palace Centre Theatre Organ Heritage Centre, where ancient cinema and theatre organs are kept, cared for and, of course played. The centre also stages film shows and is akin to a small theatre. It is open most days to the public and can be hired for private parties. Film shows of the silent film era are also shown from time to time. There is a health centre and pharmacy, kiddies' play areas, a fine primary school, builder and joinery firms, an embroidery factory (Greenlaw's largest employer) speciality candle makers, organic vegetable growers, an auction firm, furniture restorers, antique shop and the ever popular Blackadder Caravan Park which boosts the town's population for a goodly part of the year; all that is joined by so many surrounding farms which still provide employment though not so much as yesteryear. While the post office and bank have closed, vans still visit every week to provide postal and banking services.

We must not forget, the beautiful walks around the town, the woodlands and, of course, along the river and the flat track bed of the old, long gone railway, though the Station House still stands as a private home. Finally, the townspeople are truly proud of their football team's home ground at WS Happer Memorial Park set just to the west of the exit road to Coldstream, amid beautiful woodlands where many fine walks are to be had. The lands for the football pitch and woodlands were provided by the son of Mr. W.S. Happer and opened by Mrs Ann Trotter, the great man's daughter and a fine cairn was erected to remind us all of the occasion.

So many of today's people do and have done so much for the town but that, it seems, is how it has always been. If we look back over the years, there has always been someone willing to help the people. The Brounfield barons did so

~ Greenlaw – Longformacus ~

much for community, school and church over the centuries and, without that family and with much help from the Marchmont lords, Greenlaw may never have achieved its status in the highest annals of Berwickshire life and, though the days of glory have gone, there still exists a fine village and a friendly, close-knit community.

The Purves family of Purves Hall, later Marchmont, chipped in too with many benevolent acts purely for the ordinary folk with no thought of anything in return. That family were especially helpful when men returned from the wars of the 19th century, in France, Crimea and South Africa. The returning heroes had no work and no hope until the Purves family, in the person of Sir William-Purves-Hune-Campbell, stepped in and virtually created new work simply to give the men jobs. He of course, was the man who built the County Hall.

Others of note are John Fairbairn, Free Kirk Minister and founder of that church's school has become a large part of local folklore and is remembered through the hall and new housing named in his honour. He was regarded in the highest esteem not just in Greenlaw but indeed throughout Scotland. His brother Patrick, was another who went on to great things within the hierarchy of the Free Church particularly in Glasgow and many of his writings are still of importance in the modern day. We have already witnessed the benevolence of the Happer family who gave so much to the town but another, Thomas Gibson, left the people with an invaluable documentation of old Greenlaw in his book, *An Old Berwickshire Town – Greenlaw*. Another local man, Robert Young, left his memoirs in his *Road to Grinlae* which was put to book by his son. If ever there was anything going in Greenlaw, Robert was part of it, founding the electricity system and improving drinking water were two of his greatest achievements. Two ladies of the aristocrat families, Lady Brigid McEwan of Marchmont and Felicity Douglas-Home, both of good heart and benevolence, still live in the area and are still fondly greeted in the village.

Of course in the modern era, there are still good people who do so much, meaning Greenlaw will never be left on the 'starting blocks'. So many in this small town ensure all is well within the community of today as they did yesterday and will do, with others like them, the same tomorrow.

~ Longformacus - Whitchester - Ellemford ~

Just under seven miles north-west of Duns, lies the old village of Longformacus tucked neatly astride the Dye Water, in the southern reaches of the hills of Lammermuir. For centuries the little community on the Dye wore the title '*Capital of Lammermoor*' with a great deal of pride and so much respect was afforded the industrious community. Over the centuries, many families vied for the right to command the hill route north and many an angry

~ *Longformacus* ~

sword was drawn in pursuit of control of that road and the village on which it stood. During the early years, the Dunbars, Erskines, Randolphs, Douglases and the de St Clairs made claim to the parish but it was the last named, the St.Clair family of Roslin and Herdmanston who prevailed. That family were renowned for their church and castle building and there seems little doubt it was they who erected the first church at the village and, at least one tower, the remains of which can still be seen at the foot of Sinclairs Hill, near the end of Manse Road though another tower existed in early times directly opposite Rathburne House. Quite apart from the more 'modern' towers, so many ancient sites have been discovered including hill forts, enclosures and burial grounds particularly the *Mutiny Stones,* a nearly 100 yards long stone cairn full of long cists said to be from 3,000BC all affording proof positive, this region was not only well populated but one of the busiest routes, north to south from early times in what became southern Scotland

It is not clear when the de St. Clairs assumed control though some say the lands were granted them in 1384 by the Earl of Dunbar and that may well be the case, but the fact Gregory de St. Clair swore fealty, in 1296, to Edward I at Berwick on behalf of Longformacus, tends to tell us, their reign began with, or before,

Meagre remains of tower below Sinclair's Hill

that man, though there is the case, the family did have property in the area but were not the principal family until Dunbar's grant of 1384. It must be said, in those far off days, the Douglas family of Mordington, the Randolph family in the shape of the Earls of Moray and of course, the Earls of March, all had influence in the important staging post through the Lammermuirs.

There is very little reference to the early church but there seems little doubt, a chapel would be in a place lorded over by the pious de St. Clairs, their record of building chapels wherever they lived, went before them. However when we look more closely at the history of the church itself, it would appear the de St. Clairs, though prolific landowners all around the region may not have been the heritors of the early church, that honour was thought to have been held by the Douglases. However, when the church was rebuilt in 1730, burials were

~ *Longformacus* ~

found below with a stone of the St. Clairs, which leads to more speculation as to the true founders of the kirk. What appears to be the case, there may be parallel tales of who was who and who did what at Longformacus. There are many instances in old Scottish history where a parish is presided over by this family or that when in actual fact, each had parts of the parish which caused misinterpretation time after time. The best pointer we have is, what we dig out of the ground or who is mentioned by charter. In the case of Longformacus, it would appear the de St. Clair family were indeed the overlords on both counts, even though the others did have some influence in and around the parish. If further evidence was required, it arrived in 1892, when the kirk was wholly refurbished and even more bones were found with yet another Sinclair stone, all helping confirm the Sinclair family as the founders of the church. and, according to experts, the lower parts of the building was from no later than the 14th century but probably much earlier.

*T*he beautiful old kirk **(below)** built in 1730 and, at least, the third on the site, is one of the most atmospheric in Berwickshire, but has been closed for some time and completely cleared in readiness for a bold new venture, to convert the old building in to a heritage centre where the history of the church and parish can be better interpreted meaning the history of Longformacus can be handed down for generations to come. The interior of the kirk during its working life was sublime, everything an old church should be. An atmospheric nave with a raised area to the west, a laird's loft, ancient burials and stones within and the lovely chancel to the east entered below an arch with the never to be forgotten words, *Worship the Word in the beauty of Holiness*

*T*he kirkyard is equally impressive with many fine stones of all varieties including symbolic, table, urns and obelisk but the most eyecatching is the architecturally supreme burial aisle of the philanthropic local Brown family, The church was designed and built by the much respected Duns architect, George Fortune who later had a window inserted in the church in his honour.

*A*nother church, a Free Kirk, was built in the village at the disruption of

~ *Longformacus* ~

1843 when around 100 members of the established church left to join the new congregation. When the cause of the Disruption, rich men controlling the church, was 'put to bed' the parishioners returned to the fold leaving the new church redundant but happily the building has survived to the present day in the form of a private residence. A chapel existed at Rawburn near the site of the present day farmhouse but little of that chapel, if anything, is known apart from its existence. The present day farmhouse was once said to be the home of a devout Covenanter, Margaret Tunnock.

The de St. Clairs built an extremely large estate around them as their power in the area, grew. Their holding of the lordship continued through eleven generations beginning with James de St. Clair who received the lands in a charter of 1384 making it official who was the laird. The fifth of that line, James, who used the modern name of Sinclair, received the new Barony of Longformacus in a charter issued at Dunbar Castle by the Duke of Albany in 1472. His son, Alexander had the charter renewed in 1503 when the barony was so named, Lochormacus. The 11th Sinclair Laird of the lands was Robert, an advocate before the Court of Session, who was created the 1st Baronet of the lands at the hands of Charles II in 1664. The end finally came for the family when Sir John, VII Baronet died in 1843 without issue, though the family had left the estates in the previous century because of bankruptcy, part of which may have been caused by the building of Longformacus House in 1730.

John Hume purchased Longformacus House in the latter part of the 18th century before, in time, receiving an offer he could not refuse, from David Wardrop Brown. One day, a heavily tanned stranger rode in to the village and was approached by the school master, William Wanless who enquired of the stranger, his business. The horseman asked who owned the house and, having received the information he needed, promptly rode to the front door and offered Johnny Hume, as he was known to his estate workers, the sum of £30,000 in cash, a sum of money which, in the earlier part of the 19th century, would be worth several million pounds at present day values. Mr Hume, who had made significant alterations and improvements to an already stately home, accepted the offer even though with heavy heart.

Longformacus House, for long the home of the Brown family, was built at around the same time as the 18th century church and is the biggest house in the parish. It is well known for a wonderful walled garden, beautiful estate and ancient doocot. (dovecote) In 1800, David Brown of Longformacus, a qualified lawyer, helped form a great spice company in Penang, a state in Malaysia and, to this day, there are many Brown descendants in that country where their name is revered and where a great monument and wonderful gardens were built in David Brown's memory. A holy well, dedicated to Our Lady, once existed in Longformacus, and bore the inscription 1581 and the initials D. W. B., said to represent David Wardlaw Brown, but date and initials

~ *Longformacus* ~

did not appear to represent the same era.

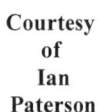

Courtesy of Ian Paterson

Longformacus House

*T*he seven bay frontage of Longformacus House, includes a three bay, projecting portico reached by steps through columned pillars across the basement, and is topped by a pyramidal pediment. The house is essentially of two floors with a full size basement and several projecting windows in the attic. Each window is sash and cased and contains eight panes. The Browns built an extension on to the south elevation but that has long since been demolished returning the old house to its former glories. The house is now described as one of the most significant houses, not only in the parish but in the entire country, a rare treasure below the Lammermuirs. The great house is reached by a long drive guarded by an impressive lodge house. Today, Longformacus Estate, now owned by the Charles family, includes several farms and is a busy and popular shooting venue.

*F*arming has always been predominant in a parish which was cojoined with the neighbouring parish of Ellem in 1712, meaning there were more areas in which a man could make an honest day's living. Around the time when the Browns took over in the first half of the 19th century, apart from farming, quarrying, corn, barley, two saw mills and a threshing machine, Longformacus also boasted cartwrights, blacksmith, two grocers, a vitner, a shoemaker and a tailor. Add that to the much sought after illicit, home made whisky, an inn and a healthy weaving industry. Their was also a thriving school and kirk making for a busy little community and clearly not 'a down at the heel settlement' as some believe. In time a telegraph office and Post office would open..

*O*f course, the Scottish Borders is very much a rural area and farms are around every corner, so many of them livestock farms. Of course much of what we eat is reared in this beautiful region but the main claim to fame is the weaving of wool and the garments which were produced and Longformacus

~ *Longformacus* ~

was no stranger to that industry and many weavers of old plied their trade in the southern Lammermuirs. Farmers are so renowned too for there fine houses and farmsteads and the village is surrounded by so many such places, farms like, Stobswood, Whinrig, Rawburn, Kippetlaw, Caldra, Horseupcleuch, Old Stobswood, Muirton, and Redpath are but a few.

*I*n the 18th, 19th and early 20th centuries, particularly during the summer season, most houses in the village...and the farms, were full of people from Duns, Haddington and further afield, keen to book a room to spend their holiday in the arms of beauty. That beauty consisted of the Watch, Dye and Whiteadder Waters, the fishing therein and the gentle beauty of the rolling hills of Lammermoor to the north and Dirrington Great Law where three great cairns dominate the peak and Dirrnington Little Law with a cairn of it is own and an atmospheric cross of 2000AD to mark a new millenium, all set in the arms of peaceful seclusion to the south. That did no harm whatsoever to the two inns at Longformacus and Ellem where many a song of the Scots' tongue was sung and bargains made between the local anglers and their guests. Angling was, and still is, so popular and the Ellem Angling Club was formed in 1827 with the later Whiteadder Angling Association founded in 1930. Of course, it was not only summer the visitors arrived, winter too, was popular with visitors and locals alike, keeping the curling pond forever busy as well as an old camping park.

*A*nother popular fishing facility was created, almost be default, when the Watch Water reservoir was opened in 1954 covering some 48 hectares and

Rathburne House – courtesy of Ian Paterson

surrounding earthen banks. That great piece of engineering was not only a great new source of fresh water for the region, it also provided more housing for Longformacus. Initially the homes were built for the workers on the reservoir but were left behind when the works were complete, providing a much needed boost to local people. In later times the village also boasted a hotel/inn, Rathburne House, a former shooting lodge, which later operated a bed a breakfast business but in the present day it is a family home. Rathburne is situated to the west of the village near the site of an ancient castle on the

~ *Longformacus* ~

banks of the Dye Water but barely a stone remains of that old fortalice.

The aforementioned school was very fortunate in as much it was endowed with several long serving schoolmasters who went above the call of duty in teaching the children of the parish. Two of those masters deserve the greatest of praise for the work they did over an incredible period of 93 years, virtually a century of dedication. Those men were George Sherriff who taught the children for 48 years through the end of the 18th century, in to the earlier part of the 19th and William Wanless, his successor, another much respected man who was in charge at the school for 45 years. It is not known when the first school opened at Longformacus but the last school, which closed in the late 1980s and is now a private home (as is the schoolmaster's house) was the third school on the site.

Essentially, the village contains just four streets, Manse Road where some beautiful old houses exist, Duns road, where lovely cottages and the Village Hall can be found, Gifford Road hosts some of the reservoir houses, more lovely bungalows and the old school and schoolmaster's house. Pride of place though goes to the The Row **(below)** a line of old estate cottages overlooking the eternal Dye Water, a row of architectural masterpieces and look out for the stork atop the apex of no. 1 which has acted as a shop, post office and the

telegraph office in bygone days. Opposite the Row and across the thoroughfare are the gardens, all in a row and covered in rainbow beauty.

Today Longformacus, on the Southern Upland Way, is still the same lovely, little village as it has always been but, sadly, with less facilities than of old meaning the children must now travel to Duns for their education. There is no inn, no school nor shops, and now no church but yet the villagers are content with their lot, the events in their fine wee hall keep them happy as does their warm welcome of the Duns Reiver and his colourful cavalcade during their ride in to the hills, a visit which also includes Whitchester, the old home of

~ *Longformacus – Whitchester* ~

Andrew Smith who, as it happens, financed the building of Longformacus Hall.

Where there are haunting hills, there are, invariably, haunting tales and, before we leave the village, I must share one with you, of the tale of the local blacksmith family, the Niels. There are several versions of this story but I shall relate the first one I heard. One day, John Niel, local blacksmith and father of the family, set out for Greenlaw to attend a funeral. On the way home over the moor, he had to ford the Foul Burn when suddenly a macabre ghostly creature atop a strange form of horse, apprehended him. The phantom figure threatened to kill him and take John for his own before the frightened man made a deal with the devilish demon. He offered one of his sons to the fiend if ever any of them crossed the burn after sunset, to which the evil creature agreed. Some years later, John's son, Henry, having concluded his business in Greenlaw, decided to return home and, even though his father had warned him of his deal with the devil, he decided to take the chance. As he approached the burn, the light faded and he was indeed overtaken by evil. His lifeless body dressed with his clothes on back to front, was found the next day, John Niel's, deal with the de'il was now concluded and a stone was later laid at the spot as a memorial and a stern reminder, never cross that Foul Ford after sunset!

- *Whitchester* -

On we go to Ellemford but before that, we must visit Whitchester House, once home to the great and philanthropic Andrew Smith. In 1878, Andrew Smith and his wife, Ida bought Whitchester and spent the next few years converting the old farm house into a sublime work of art. From the moment of that couple's arrival, life, for everyone in the parish, and beyond, changed for the better. Over the years, the new laird funded great changes, not only for Longformacus Church where he financed great renovation, and rebuilding including a new west aisle and the atmospheric apse to the east. Just a few years later, he provided the funds for the building of the new kirk at Cranshaws; built a small hospital and chapel at Whitchester and provided the funds for the creation of the Duns public park and gateway to the park before building Longformacus Village Hall. Such a wonderfully generous man, long will his name be remembered with great affection in the southern foothills of the Lammermuirs.

Andrew, and his good wife Ida, also provided the funds to build Whitchester Hospital in Duns in the dying days of the 19th century; the hospital later became known as Haymount Hospital situated in Trinity Lane off Bridgend and while that hospital is long closed, it still exist as a private residence. So much gratitude is owed that generous couple and they are rightly deserving of the their place in the annals of Duns and can rightly take their

~ *Whitchester* ~

place at the 'top table'

Andrew and his family made their fortunes in brewing when he was in partnership with the famous Younger brewing family in Edinburgh, but when he reached the southern reaches of Scotland, his thoughts turned to farming and of course, helping others.. When Andrew died in 1914, he left the world a better place, but so much the poorer on his passing. Interestingly, Whitchester Farm was, in days long gone, a house of the Cistercian Nuns of Coldstream and Eccles.

The principal entrance to Whitchester House

In the modern day, most of the great gardens have gone as has the vast array of greenhouses but in recent times, during a dig, a section of garden was uncovered. The house has, in recent times been used as a rehabilitation centre in the Teen Challenge organisation and provides a very Christian role on an estate which was owned as we saw, by the Cistercians. Therefore the great house and estate still acts as a place of goodness for which Andrew and Ida Smith would have been so proud but the centre of today is not the first use since the leaving of the Smiths. It has played its part in many fine projects over the century plus since the couple died, such as a school and chapel for the residents in need of help and that is still the case in the present day where Bible study and prayer is still a very essential part of the curriculum. It is difficult to find anywhere, a lay institution such as Whitchester, which has become an institution, where so much goodness has been afforded so many for so long. Andrew and Ida Smith, are two of the most revered Scots and this small part of southern Scotland is surely so blessed and privileged to have had them in their midst, even to the present day where their legacy is still helping others in need.

~ *Ellemford* ~

Before entering Ellemford from the west, there exists a very fine roadside house standing as it does, as a great white beacon, overlooking the Whiteadder Water as if ensuring all below is in a safe pair of hands. That lovely old house is merely a forerunner of what is to come, from Rigfoot Farm in to the hamlet itself, stands the most wonderful array of lovely houses and cottages, all the way to the Duns - Gifford road. The houses, at the bottom of the hill, are the oldest and feature the Old Ellem Inn, Ellem Lodge and Woodside Cottage, all works of art in their own right. Just round the corner, on the Duns Road, stands Ellembank Cottage on or very near, the site of the famed Mrs. Mack's Cottage, while further south is the inspiring Whitchester Lodge. Across the river, spanned by the 19th century bridge, another wonderful house, cloaked in white, is Todlaw, standing as a sentry to the hamlet's, 'northern yett' while up the hill is the great Ellemford Estate House, a beautifully converted family house owned by the Wilson family, the local lairds, some farm cottages and finally, Green Hope, a beautiful house, deserving of its place at the top of the hill overlooking a lovely valley. The house is also used as a bed and breakfast establishment and is home to the Landale family who once owned the entire estate.

Ellemford Estate House
Courtesy of David Spry

Because of its situation, Ellemford was always a busy route in times gone by, on the north, south thoroughfare. It was a direct route between Scotland and England but it was also a route of the 'unseen'. This was a *Paradise Way*, for those who feared detection like, whisky bootleggers, criminals, vagabonds and beggars. The 'unwanted' rarely travelled during daylight hours, their times of travel was usually under the cover of dark skies above even darker hills. Of course others travelled the route for every day use and business or even sight seeing, it is a lovely route through hills and past the Whiteadder Reservoir.

Of course others too have travelled the hill route, from the first known man, and so many ancient enclosures have been found, to bishops and their chaplains, kings and courtiers followed by great armies. Indeed, a great army of Scots assembled there in 1496 with plans to invade England but for one

~ *Ellemford* ~

reason or another no invasion was made. However, in the days leading up to Scotland's darkest moment, another great army assembled at Ellemford, when the forces of King James IV of Scots, gathered there in August, 1513, when the great army knelt below the old kirk to receive the blessings of the local parson and the king's personal chaplain as they prepared to invade England in the cause of cementing the *Auld Alliance* with France. Many others from across the Borders and the rest of Scotland arrived to join the battalions who had trudged over the Lammermuirs after prayers were offered at St. Giles in Edinburgh and St. Mary's at Haddington before the march through Nunraw and across the daunting hills.

As we have already intimated, the king's army prevailed in the early stages of the campaign and several castles were destroyed but, when they took the extra step near Branxton, on the fields near Flodden, a nation's youth and much of the aristocracy perished with their King.

*K*ing James IV had a great liking for Ellemford, at least twice between the two occasions his army assembled there, he returned on hunting trips and stayed at a house in the parish. In 2013, a dramatised walk was held to mark the 500th anniversary of the tragic battle. A large group of enthusiasts met at Nunraw and from start to finish, were greeted by local actors who virtually took them along every footstep of the king's and his army's fateful journey south. At the end of the special march south, The *In the Footsteps of Flodden* group all picked a stone and laid them all together to form a cairn on the haugh to the west of the Ellemford Bridge, to mark the anniversary of a sad occasion.

*O*f course, the kirk, below which the king and his army were blessed, was in fact, one of the oldest churches in Scotland and was thought to have been established by Patrick of Dunbar and his wife, Ada, daughter of William I (The Lion) in the late 12th century. It was they who founded the priories at Eccles and Coldstream and had major input in to the foundation of Cistercians as was the case at nearby Whitchester and and of course, at Abbey St. Bathans.

*S*adly, we do not have too much information on the early church but that may be because it was a daughter house of the Chapel Royal at Stirling for some time. What we do know is, Henri de Ellem, almost certainly the parson, travelled to Berwick in 1296 to pay his homage to Edward I and of Parson Thomas Brown who begged Edward III to return his church after the fateful Battle of Homildon Hill in 1366. Sandwiched between those dates was the visit of Bishop, David de Bernham of St. Andrews, who arrived in the southern Lammermuirs to consecrate the church on the 11th March, 1243. The good bishop never consecrated new churches, only the older, more established kirks thus giving us another clue to the antiquity of the old divine at Ellem. In 1712, the old church was falling in to serious disrepair and was, that year, united with the church at Longformacus. The last minister before the church closed was the Rev. John Brown who held the cure for 24 years until his death in 1712.

~ *Ellemford* ~

*O*ver the years, the historic church has been allowed to fritter away to a shell and die. Today barely a fragment remains and only a few headstones of the ones who once worshipped within the hallowed walls of a now ruinous church which is situated on the left bank of the Whiteadder, on the hill and enshrouded behind trees. Recent digs have been made at the site but, apart from a few stones and human remains, nothing else of significance was found.

*E*llem has, for centuries, been a popular destination not only for kings and vagabonds but for the hunting enthusiast and still is! Not only was an old inn, Ellem Cottage, a popular meeting place in those early days, the Ellem Inn was even more popular in later times. Today, shooting enthusiasts as we shall see, still descend on the estate where they are admirably catered for at the old Ellemford Farmhouse and at Green Hope.

Ellemford Bridge with Ellem Lodge in the background

The Whiteadder is a busy water being a magnet for fishermen from all parts joining members of the Ellem Fishing Club which is the oldest such club in the world having been founded before 1827 as indicated at Longformacus.

*O*f course in earlier times, the Whiteadder was not always simply for sport, fish were exported to more busy centres thus allowing local fishermen and their families to put a roof over their heads and food on the table. One of the most important houses at that point was the aforementioned Ellem Cottage, now part of Ellem Lodge and, in 1852, it was reported that *James Rae has taken possession of the excellent fishing quarters, so well suited for Gentlemen fishing the Whiteadder.* That report indicated the cottage was used as a fishing tavern but was previously thought to have been be the local Toll House. That old building is now an integral part of Ellem Lodge which was

~ *Ellemford* ~

built as a round building in the late 18th century and is similar in style to the Retreat at Abbey St. Bathans, but is now cojoined with the fishing tavern with further, later additions, to form one of the most beautiful, and unusual houses in the region, simply unique. It is so unique, it even had a toilet building in the trees with a path leading directly from the front door. Ellem Lodge was featured during the BBC's fascinating documentary series, *The House Detectives* when they deduced the age of the house and if there had been any earlier structures but none were found. Ellem Inn, probably built even earlier than the lodge, still hovers majestically across the road from Woodside Cottage which was transformed from the old forester's house in 1894 by Ida Florence Landale. That old house proudly boasts an unusual, cubed sundial.

**Ellembank Cottage in the grounds of Mrs. Mack's Cottage
Courtesy of David Spry**

Betty Mack was an interesting worthy, not only did she own the local sawmill, across the Duns Road from her cottage, she also purveyed local whisky which, during her time, was legal but as we have seen, that benefit soon disappeared but she carried on regardless.

Quarrying too was extremely important along with the time honoured farming industry with wool from the sheep, the most important produce. Wool meant weaving industries and that was carried out for centuries at the fast flowing river from her source in Lammermuir to her confluence with the River Tweed. Oats and barley too, were produced and a large cereal export industry existed in early times meaning busy roads with the constant carting to and from the busy port at Dunbar. Sawmills too, as we have seen, were kept 'on their toes'. There were a couple of household grocers in the village including one at Mrs. Mack's house where, no doubt, liquor was on the menu.

Another industry which was carried out for some considerable time was copper mining though the poor returns put an end to that. Everything has gone

~ *Ellemford* ~

now with the exception of the eternal farming, and fishing but now only for sport. A smiddy was kept busy for centuries too but has gone forever, lost in the annals of local history though the smith's house and workshop still exist, looking a lost and forlorn 'building at risk' on the right bank of the Whiteadder on Ellemhaugh, a little distance to the north-west of the hamlet. A local sawmill however, still thrives against all the odds.

Ellemford is to still the place to be if you wish an away from it all, activity holiday, and the region provides everything the outdoor enthusiast could wish for. Across the bridge, on the left bank of the Whiteadder Water, is Ellemford Estate, one of the most popular sporting estates in Scotland. The estate is a centre of outdoor sports par excellence including shooting, fishing, deer stalking and much more. Ellemford offers the peace and quiet for a relaxing holiday, where accommodation is provided, not only for the sports and walking on the estate which covers 3,000 acres, but also those who wish to visit the towns and villages, explore Berwickshire and the wider Border region or search for some of the most testing golf courses known to man. It is one of the finest estates of its kind in Scotland where everything required is offered, and where no stone is left unturned in their efforts to ensure the whole experience is as enjoyable as can possibly be.

The small hamlet is the home of a show which has been held every year for well over a century and is still going strong. Organised by the Lammermuir Pastoral Society, the show features all things sheep, from sheep dog trials to the judging of all breeds with so many trophies up for grabs. There is too, an industrial section where everything from tractors to ploughs are shown. Many side stalls, which are certain to be of interest to visitors and farmers alike, are on site in league with the many food outlets available to whet the appetite of the hundreds who attend the show every year. The dog trials is part of the overall Scottish Sheep Dog Trials circuit. That show is held each year in September, on the site of an old picnic and caravan park on the left bank.

The old caravan and picnic area

Courtesy of David Spry

~ Ellemford – Polwarth ~

*I*n the present day, Ellemford is just a little bit sleepier than it was in the old days, no longer do people arrive looking for illicit whisky nor without their proof of identity. The days of the vagabond and warring men have happily gone, leaving the tiny community at peace with itself and the world outside. There are no facilities whatsoever, if you omit the local red telephone box and the letter box but, while the local community do not have what the rest of us take for granted, they do possess something we all crave for from time to time throughout our lives...peace and quiet, in their very own little piece of heaven.

~ Polwarth ~

*T*oday's 'village' of Polwarth is nothing more than a pale shadow of its former self, with only a few scattered houses barely worthy of the name hamlet never mind village. Gone are the rows of cottages leading up to the Kirk Burn, gone too is the inn, the schools and shops; there is very little work and even the proud and ancient old kirk has closed meaning anyone who wishes to attend Sunday service or anything else for that matter, must travel, west to Greenlaw or east to Gavinton or Duns.

*T*he old Kirk of Polwarth, dedicated to St. Mungo, has been closed for some years now and more recently has been sold in to private ownership. In her book of 1894, *Marchmont and the Humes of Polwarth,* Margaret Warrender, a member of the eminent Polwarth family, relates there has been a place of worship on the site for more than a thousand years, while a plaque at the church appears to confirm that statement, though others are convinced a chapel was in place long before the 9th century. Though no concrete evidence has been found to substantiate their claims, there is absolutely no reason whatsoever to dispute those assertions. One thing is for certain, the church at Polwarth is, no doubt one of the very early places of worship in Berwickshire. The new

The old Kirk of Polwarth

~ Polwarth ~

owners of the church wish to maintain the building in a fashion so it may be used for the occasional service or wedding in the future.

While we know of no one in 9th century Polwarth, there are many names known to us from the early 12th century onwards. We know of two Adams, father and son, of Polwarth who received lands in Beath Fleming in Fife, a gift which was witnessed by many of the local aristocracy including Constantine of Lochore, the son of David, Lord Strathbogie and others. They later gifted lands at Dunipace near Falkirk perhaps giving us a glimpse of the early lords at Polwarth in the late 12th and early 13th century. Another of some note, Beatrice, wife of Robert of Polwarth, is known by a charter of Kelso, to have exchanged some lands at Wedderlie in the mid 13th century. Patrick, son and brother of the aforementioned Adams of Polwarth made a further gift of lands at Dunipace around 1258. Robert, husband of the above, Beatrice, made further grants of Wedderlie, to the monks of Kelso Abbey.

Another important occasion from the 13th century arrived in 1242 when His Eminence, Bishop David de Bernham, dedicated the old divine in the name of St. Kentigern or Mungo as the great man was otherwise known. In 1296, parson Adam Lambe swore fealty to King Edward before, three years later, the same king presented William de Sandystone as rector of the Church of Paulesworth. In July, 1304, Patrick of Polwarth was another who paid homage to Edward I of England and was subsequently imprisoned but released on the death of the English despot in 1307.

By 1378, the church was described as ruinous and the the family did not have the means to reinstate the building though Sir Patrick's son-in-law, Johannes de St. Clair of Hermanstoun, came to the rescue by providing the funds to re-build the old lady. A tablet above the main entrance confirms the generosity and piousness of the good Johannes de St. Clair, husband of Elizabeth Hume, only child of Sir Patrick. When Sir Patrick died, Johannes became the laird of, not only Polwarth but also the estates of Kimmerghame. The St. Clairs then refurbished and strengthened Polwarth Castle, a castle which was later destroyed during the English raids in the mid 1540s during the so called Wars of the Rough Wooing.

On the death of John de St. Clair, the estates passed down the line to his great-grandson, John Sinclair who died in the late 15th century without male issue meaning Polwarth and Kimmerghame passed to his brother, Sir William of Herdmanston. On his death, the lands were left to his two daughters, Marion and Margaret who married two brothers, George and Patrick Hume of Wedderburn, Marion to George who became laird and lady of Wedderburn and Margaret to Patrick being entitled 'of Polwarth and Kimmerghame'. The weddings took place at Polwarth Kirk before a great celebration on the Green, with much merriment around the Thorn. The Polwarth branch of the family lived for a while at the old Maines House near Chirnside, before returning

~ *Polwarth* ~

to Polwarth at Redbraes Castle and later to Marchmont.

In the wake of the Reformation, Adam Hume, 3rd son of the 4th Baron of Polwarth became the first minister of the reformed kirk at Polwarth in 1567 following a period of readers at the church. The reasons for having readers of course was, when the Reformation arrived in 1560, there were literally no ministers, or at best, very few and, until enough ministers could be educated in the new Calvinist faith, lay members of the congregation conducted the services.

In the 17th century, the population was increased when a number of Walloon and French Huguenots arrived in the parish fleeing persecution in their own countries. They too had embraced the teaching of John Calvin and, like the Scots, they too denounced Roman Catholic ways. They brought with them at least one new industry, tanning, which became an important source of work to the local people which blended in well with the established local shoe making industry.

Bell of 1697 in Polwarth Kirk courtesy of Becky Williamson

1703 saw the building of the present Church on the same site as the older buildings and much of those early edifices are contained in the 'new' building which, architecturally and historically, is regarded as one of the most significant buildings in Scotland. The church is built of rubblestone, from local quarries, below a grey-slated roof. The 'T' shaped building is highlighted by a four-stage tower and the interior was extensively restored in the 20th century. Below the eastern section of the north wall, there is the crypt of the Marchmont family which can still be seen through grills at the lower stage of the wall. That crypt not only contains the coffins of members of the family but an interesting piece of Berwickshire history.

The so called *'Rye House Plot'* of 1683, an attempt on the assassination of the much detested Charles II and his brother, James, Duke of York, was detected and the conspirators sought by the Crown. Sir Patrick Home of Polwarth was implicated and hid in the crypt of Polwarth Church for four weeks to where his daughter, Grizell, brought him food and water. Lady Grizell Home's (later Baillie) well trodden path became known as the 'Lady's Walk'. Her daily walks from Redbraes Castle saved her father's life and helped him achieve great position and acclaim after the fall of James VII and the Glorious Revolution in England in 1688. Some years later, the family built the Palladian style Marchmont House, details of which we have seen.

While the Polwarth of today is so quiet, it was not always like that, it was a place of merriment and parties were constantly held on the green where

~ *Polwarth* ~

couples danced round the renowned Polwarth Thorn Bush. Even more wonderful occasions included weddings when the happy couples sealed their union by dancing round the bush; when old friends reunited or indeed any celebration at all, they invariably ended up at the Thorn. So many songs were written over the years by some great poets including Allan Ramsay. One verse from one of the many versions reads :

> *At Polwarth on the Green*
> *If you'll meet me in the morn*
> *Where lads and lassies do convene*
> *To dance around the Thorn*

In those happy times, as intimated, the village contained everything required to sustain a small farming community where all their food was available at the various farms or shops. There were, throughout the 19th century, two schools, the parish and a girls only school with the parish school surviving well in to the following century. A railway station existed at Marchmont Estate which opened in 1850 but closed just over 100 years later though the platform and railway house, now a private residence, can still be seen. There were also two grocers, a tippling inn, shoe makers, two stone masons, a miller, a joiner and a blacksmith. A little quarrying took place, mainly for dyking and local cottages of which there were more than a few. The people though were, by far, gainfully employed on the farms or, as we have seen, tanning the local leather.

An old postcard of a street full of cottages at Polwarth courtesy of Lee Davies

~ *Polwarth – Swinton & Simprim* ~

They knew how to enjoy themselves too when work was done and many fêtes and parties were held throughout the year but the highlights were the two fairs in the village but more particularly St. Mungo's Fair which was enacted annually for centuries on the Feast Day of St. Mungo (Kentigern) King James V is said to have visited the fair and may even have danced around the famous Polwarth Thorn. At one such fair, an argument was ignited on a disagreement between two of the packmen, an argument which became so violent, it resulted in one of them being killed and to this day the spot is marked on the Packman's Brae leading to the church.

Times were, more than often difficult, to say the least but the poor of the community were luckier than many others in the Borders thanks to the 6th Baronet of Marchmont, Sir William-Purves-Hume-Campbell. That benevolent man did all he could to help the less than lucky. Those who were infirm or disabled, and those who could not find employment in the region were taken care of by the kindly laird, who, as at Greenlaw, provided food for the table and a roof over their heads. He also provided funds for the children to have clothes to wear and shoes for their feet, even purchasing books to assist with their education.

Those times are long gone but the sleepy hamlet lives on though much, much smaller than before but still the old church overlooks proceedings from high above the Kirk Burn from where the baptismal waters were once drawn.

The remnants of the village of Polwarth and its church will dwell long, even if only to serve as a reminder of more fulfilling days in the history of Berwickshire...and beyond.

As a note of interest, the original title of the Humes of Redbraes or Marchmont, was Lord Polwarth which they later held along with the title, Earl of Marchmont. Though the Earl title has long since became extinct, the title of Lord Polwarth lives on in the shape of Andrew Walter Hepburne-Scott, the 11th Lord who lives at the family seat at Harden. His heir apparent is his son, the Hon. William Henry Hepburne-Scott, Master of Polwarth. Many of that particular family were buried in the family vault at Old Mertoun Kirk.

~ *Swinton with Simprin* ~

There has been a settled community at Swinton from early medieval times, and it is reasonable to believe a church would arrive early considering the route on which the village lay, between Lindisfarne and Melrose, a route travelled by so many of the early apostles as they headed north spreading the good word as they went. So often, they founded a place of worship and it is certainly possible that was the case at Swinton. Since we know the church at Swinton was in place before 1098AD, it is obvious, the community of

~ *Swinton* ~

Swinewood, or Swinton, was already in place before that time. In fact, many people strongly believe there was a place of worship at Swinton from the days of Saint Cuthbert who lived his entire life in the 7th century. While that may well be the case, we have absolutely no proof whatsoever of such a foundation.

*1*098 is a pivotal year in the history of Swinton since that was the year in which King Edgar, son of Malcom III, granted the church and village to Coldingham. The king's words upon confirmation to Coldingham were : "*Villam totam Swinton cum divisis, sicut Liulf habuit*" That is 'the village of Swinton, the place where Liulf lives' That charter of grant to Coldingham was not however, the first known mention of Swinton. Some years earlier, Liulf's father, Edulph or Ædulph of Northumbria, was granted the lands of Swinewood by Edgar's father, Malcolm III (Canmore) who died in 1093, in return for his help in restoring the king's throne after several wars in the north of Scotland. Liulf was considered, the 1st Lord of Swinton but the first man ever to be knighted in Scotland, was another Edulph or Ernulf, son of Liulf, who was knighted by David I in 1136. That proud moment arrived at Haddington Palace when the king reconfirmed the grant of lands and church of Swinton to Coldingham Priory with reference to his knight, Ernulf, lord of those lands. (*Charters. David I. no. 53)* That further confirmed Swinton's situation within the see of Coldingham which all tends to tell us, the church like the lands, is definately pre-1093 making it, in terms of what we know, "one of the oldest churches in Berwickshire" I have to say, so many other kirks have been mentioned as 'one of the oldest' but, in the case of Swinton, the proof of existence comes from actual charters of the time.

*T*he Swinton famly can trace their roots accurately to nearly two centuries before the the Norman Conquest of England, most notably, yet another, Edulph, chief of the family, when he accepted Alfred the Great as his true leader in 886AD. Edulph was part of a great family of overlords in Northumbria which included the family of Cospatric future Earls of Dunbar, March and of Home. The very name, Swinton, has enlightened much of our history, fighting with great dignity and passion throughout the Wars of Independence and Succession and for France, the *'Auld Ally'*, in their centuries long war against England; the Swinton name has indeed risen high in the annals of warfare and bravery throughout the centuries right up to more modern times. The early family of Swinton also became, as their power and fame grew, great progenitors of many other notable Scottish families including the illustrious families of Gordon and Elphinstone.

*S*o many members of that great family and others of Swinton, are known from medieval times, some of whom we have already mentioned but others, having been noted in various charters include, Cospatric and his son, Alan, who swore fealty at Berwick in 1296 in the company of William the vicar; another Alan Swinton and his wife Beatrice with Eustace of Swinton, their

~ *Swinton* ~

Grieve, are mentioned in charters of the 13th century. Another known early vicar at the church, though not a Swinton, was William Bertram in 1455.

Though the Swintons wielded much power, they appeared to use their powers in the most benevolent ways. From the beginning, the family always fought on the side of 'right' whether it was at the aforementioned troubles or in the defence of the Scottish Church during the Bishop's Wars, they were bold and single minded in their quest for goodness and honesty. They proved to be great statesmen too including men who reached the higher echelons of Scottish justice and governance. Powerful families though, no matter how good, were always someone else's target but this family took every step to retain their own safety building fortified homes at Cranshaws, Mersington, Stevenson in Peeblesshire and, of course, at Swinton.

Their family home at Swinton, was greatly rebuilt in 1800 after a great fire of 1797 though it is the thought, a section of the old house is still incorporated on the south-west wing of the great mansion house which was sold to the McNab family in 1884. As we have already noted, Scotland's oldest landed family now live at Kimmerghame House while many, of course, have dispersed across the globe.

The *Queen of the Merse* as Swinton is known, grew gently over the centuries in the caring arms of the local lairds but warring men were forever passing through, or nearby, until the stage was reached when a defensive moat or fosse was created around the church to provide some protection. While many attacks were made by the English, the saddest and most poignant moment in the history of Swinton was when the local people witnessed the return of bedraggled footmen returning home from the debacle that was Flodden in 1513. The church bell, the oldest in Berwickshire, tolled in lament to our gallant young men. The Flodden Bell as it is now known, is engraved, telling all and sundry *'Maria est monem meum, 1499'* - (Mary is my name, 1499)

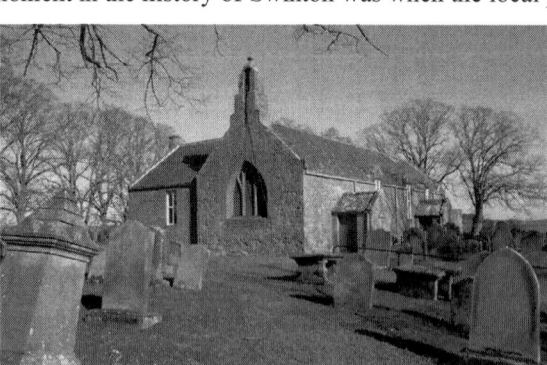

Swinton Parish Church
Courtesy of Walter Baxter

The old kirk of Swinton, first mentioned, as we have seen, in the late 11th century though the church literature, overviewing the history of the kirk, also makes a compelling case for very early worship in the village.

184

~ *Swinton* ~

The present church was much rebuilt in 1729 but parts of the foundations and sections of the north and east walls were retained from a much earlier building which had been largely restored in 1593 following at least four English attacks in barely a century. An aumbry, (recess or cupboard for holding ecclesiastical vessels) from pre-Reformation times can still be seen on the east wall.

The building, originally a long rectangle, is now of a 'T' shape, a north aisle, the Feuers' Aisle was added by the heritors in 1782 and a further northern extension was added in the 19th century giving the church four 'gables' - an original stone is built in to the wall containing all the heritors names in the Feuers' Aisle.

The pulpit **(right)** is raised and is to the west of an arcaded recess containing the effigy of one of the Swinton family, Alan Swinton, knight of that ilk. A burial vault was found under the chancel area and is certain to be the resting place of several of the local lord's family, including Alan. The raised chancel also supports the lectern and communion table and is entered by two of the most wonderfully carved timber, octagonal pillars depicting boars' heads on top. In fact there are motifs and carvings of boars all over the church, inside and out, all confirming the Laird's crest and why they were thought to gain the lands, by driving out the wild boar or swine from the district.

Apart from the crests, there is evidence of the eminent Swintons everywhere you look including the graveyard which contains many ancient stones, table and symbolic and, more Swinton burial grounds with more memorials inside and of course, the Laird's Loft. There are many other memorials in the beautiful church including those to ministers of the past and to the fallen of the Great War. Overall, Swinton Church is an uplifting place, where there is a lovely feeling of warmth which is is quite overwhelming.

The church is linked with Fogo and share the same minister, the much respected Reverend Alan Cartwright who has been minister for nearly 40 years, a remarkable commitment to the united parish. Sadly as numbers fall, there is only one Sunday service every month though Mr Cartwright,

~ *Swinton* ~

remarkably, also takes care of the congregations of Leitholm, Ladykirk and Whitsome. There is however a vibrant and enthusiastic session at the kirk.

*I*n 1843, as we know, many ministers of the church, with their elders, walked out of the General Assembly and the people of Swinton participated in that disruption and soon built a new church for the breakaway Free Kirk on the Coldstream Road. However, that church was closed after only 17 years (though remains as a private home and later known as the Fidler's Ha') when a new, more impressive, building was built at the north end of the green where it remains. In 1929, much of the Free Kirk returned to the fold and that church closed to become, in later times, the village hall.

*B*etween the years 1700 and 1755, there was a marked increase in population and housing became a more pressing matter meaning a new, planned village, one of the earliest in Scotland, was built around a large village green dominated by a town or market cross. Many say the cross is a memorial to the killing of the boars, and that is depicted, but it is more likely the cross is indeed, a market cross signifying Swinton's right to hold fairs on the third Thursday of June every year with another annual fair taking place on the fourth Tuesday in October. Nowadays, the cross is more noticeable as it sits on the centre spot of the football pitch laid out on the green and is often depicted as the 'twelfth man'. Another great occasion was the opening of the Church of Scotland School, which was later joined, for many years, by a Free Kirk School. Towards the end of the 19th century, three schools operated for a time, when a new parish council school joined the other two and, for a time, they all operated in the same building which still plays host to the children's primary education before they make their way to Berwickshire High School in Duns for their secondary education.

*M*any lovely cottages and houses look on to the green but it is so much different from the scene depicted from the 18th to the 20th centuries when the village had many shops including three grocers, a butcher, baker, tailors, shoemaker, brewer, cooper, dressmakers, a post office and hotel most set around the green and the Morningbank Inn a little to the north. There were all the trades associated with village and farm including smiths, carpenters and several quarries. The village also boasted two doctors, a police station,

~ Swinton ~

a library, reading room, football club, curling club, horticultural society and quoiting club. Some business survived for most of the 20th century and some in to the 21st century but now, all that remains is the popular Wheatsheaf Inn **(across)** on the north side of the green, two garage businesses, a gas business and what appears to be an agricultural haulage and storage depot. While there are no longer any shops in Swinton, a fish and chip van arrives every Thursday when the kids, and of course, mums and dads, can enjoy a little treat without the need to travel further afield though the villagers do wish they had a little general store.

One of the present day problems I am told, though by no means the only one, many houses lie empty for most of the year and are simply used as holiday homes, a situation which does nothing for the security and well being of the village. The homes which are occupied all year round, don't of course, all face the green and there are many fine houses, social and private, all around, with the Main Street and the Berwick, Duns and Coldstream roads all providing a varying assortment of architecture some of which is very fine indeed, it really is a lovely little village, and quite unique in the Scottish Borders.

Thankfully, the church is still open for worship and a fine primary school is well attended and where so much of the village activity takes place. The green is well used, for football and other sports including the annual school sports. Villagers once looked forward every year to their Summer Festival which took place annually with the crowning of the *Queen of the Merse* on the gala day which was held on the third Saturday of June but sadly that wonderful festival has been dormant for a number of years. The village hall has closed, for the time being and is being reassessed at the present time. There are however, several groups still managing to meet, like kids groups, an over 60s club and a horticultural society.

Agriculture was always important, and still is, though on a much reduced scale while watermills and windmills which ground out the fruits of the soil are no more than a distant memory. As mentioned, many quarries provided the

**The Cross and old Free Kirk beyond
Courtesy of Walter Baxter**

~ *Swinton - Simprim* ~

rock for buildings all over the Borders but most of those have closed though the historic Swinton Quarry still survives after being in 'cold storage' for over 60 years. The quarry is renowned for producing very fine stone and was used in the Hall of Remembrance at Edinburgh Castle and old Ladykirk Church.

Notable people include so many of the ancient Swinton family who were so benevolent over the centuries. The names of other notable people of the parish are emblazoned on the fine cairn which is the Parish War Memorial opposite the church at the junction of the Berwick and Coldstream roads but one man, Daniel Laidlaw of Little Swinton, was awarded the highest award possible, the Victoria Cross for his gallantry during the Battle of Loos in 1915. While he did not die on the field, he was wounded, his bag piping influence inspired the soldiers around him to greater things. Daniel died at Norham in 1950 and is buried at St. Cuthbert's church in that Northumbrian village. Directly across from the Memorial is a tree which was planted to celebrate the Queen's Diamond Jubilee in 2012.

~ *Simprim* ~

The former parish of Simprin was united with Swinton in the 18th century but sadly, the old village of Simprin is now a distant memory but one of its great claims to fame was, being the charge of Thomas Boston, the ground breaking minister who spread the good word there between 1699 and 1707 before his transfer to Ettrick.

It was never a large parish being the smallest in Berwickshire and, it's said in the entire country but, as we are about to find out, it was an important part of the county where many men vied for supremacy. The earliest known mention of the parish arrived in 1153 in the medium of Hye de Simpring who gifted the already existent church to Kelso Abbey and from that time until 1165 continued to grant lands to the same House of Tironesian monks as did his son, Peter. In later times, Walter de Simpring and his wife Cecilia granted lands to Coldingham and later assured the Prior there would be no further claim made by them to the said lands. Around the same time, mid 13th century, another man, Adam Lamb, almost certainly the vicar of the church, gifted lands to the house of Graden in Roxburghshire. It is believed, Adam Lamb of Simprim was the same man who was transferred to Polwarth and paid homage to Edward I 1296. In 1247, Simprim Church was blessed by consecration, an act carried out by David de Bernham, Bishop of St. Andrews. During his tenure as lord of the manor, Hye de Sympring often welcomed, Thorald, the Archdeacon of Lothian, who enjoyed his visits to Hye's home and the church so much so, he asked the Abbot of Kelso to protect his rights of visitation to the small parish.

. Hye was said to be a munificent laird and was sadly lamented when he

~ *Simprim* ~

died leaving his estate at Sympring to his son Peter, who confirmed his intentions to be as generous and liberal as his father before him. Peter's intentions were received warmly and ratified by King William I in 1213AD.

While the church and lands were in the oversee of Kelso, they, unusually, never supplied a vicar to the church, preferring to employ a clerk, used as a chaplain, to do the reading at the church though, from time to time, a qualified chaplain did offer Holy Communion. In the ancient Taxatio, Simprim

Remains of Simprim Kirk – Walter Baxter

was valued at only 15 marks but that did not prevent the Cockburns of Langton from buying the entire parish. They were the landlords through the reforming period and beyond but, because of debts, were forced to sell in 1758. Simprim was annexed to the parish of Swinton only three years later and the church with, at that time, a still used graveyard was allowed to fall in to decay, yet only a few years earlier, a new bell, weathercock and steeple had been added to the church. The bell was removed to Swinton House where it remained until 1854 when it was installed at Duns in the Christ Church, Scottish Episcopal Church.

Cottages at Simprim Mains help hold on to an ancient name

~ Simprim – Whitsome ~

Today, Simprim Kirk is a sad looking old building with very little remaining above ground. The gravestones, some of which were very fine, are lying flat while others appear to be sinking out of sight. The council do look after grass cutting and there is an interpretation board allowing visitors to read of the church's history but nonetheless it all looks so dismal. Standing on the spot, seeing the graves of loved ones of so long ago fade away in the confines of hallowed ground, as if they never existed. I find it all so heartbreaking but such is life and now, one of the smallest churches in the smallest parish in the Borders has all but gone, disappearing in the never ending march of time leaving the farm and associated buildings as the last marker on the map of a proud and ancient parish.

~ Whitsome with Hilton ~

In the mid to late 19th century, Whitsome appeared to be a prosperous, if small, village and the list of services in the community was very impressive. Apart from a church, a meeting hall and well attended parochial school, the village contained a post office, two inns, three grocers, a vitner, three dressmakers, a tailor, shoemaker, blacksmith, mason, two carpenters and all the other trades required of a rural settlement. Today, there is a motor repair garage and a wonderful community shop and post office based within the new village hall, the *Whitsome Ark.*.There is also a fruit and vegetable supplier of the highest order with a farm shop and a skip hire and waste disposal business, while all else has disappeared in the passage of time

The Ark, opened in 2009 by the Lord Lieutenant of Berwickshire, Major Alexander Richard Trotter, contains all the facilities required of the community including meeting rooms, function hall, well equipped kitchen and a café. In the modern days of centralisation, cuts and austerity, the community at Whitsome have managed to buck the trend with the opening of their beautiful, ultra modern village hall and shop, which replaced the old hall which still exists just outside the village, to the east on the Allanton Road.

The name of the parish appears to derive from huite, meaning white and ham mean settlement or home. The lairds named themselves Huite or, on occasion, Qhuite or the 'Whites' of Whitsome, who were locally powerful during medieval times. One Huite or White, was witness to King Edgar's original charter of the church. More lands in the vicinity, were owned by the powerful Hoppringle family and constant feuding took place between the Whites and Pringles, in their quest for supremacy of the parish. In time however, the lands came in to the possession of the Lyle family but that appeared to be short lived. When Robert Bruce was crowned at Scone on the 25th March, 1306 - the Annunciation Day of the Blessed Mary, he decided he

~ *Whitsome* ~

must rid the country of men who supported John de Baliol, the puppet king of Scotland, and Edward of England. Among those men was John de Yle or Lyle of Whitsome who was made forfeit and the lands returned to the Pringles. members of the eminent Smailholm and Torwoodlee family.

The Whitsome Ark a Community Centre, shop & Post Office

*T*here was however, much activity at Whitsome long before the tenure of the Huites and Lyles with many signs of a prehistoric nature and a large area which was later occupied by the invading Romans who were thought to have built a fortalice at Battle Knowes. Many finds of various forms of artefacts, military and civilian have been found there over the years; one particularly important find of an ancient burial site was made at Doons Law near the source of the Leet Water. Other lands in the parish have been attributed to the Poor Fellow Soldiers of Christ and of the Temple of Solomon or the Knights Templar as they became known; that on its own would almost certainly mean another chapel or temple for their own use.

*F*arming was, and still is, the single most important industry in the parish since the Agricultural Revolution of the 18th century, but has now become much reduced. The further coming of the 19th century Industrial Revolution when more sophisticated farm machinery and tractors were being produced meant even less jobs. In more recent times farms have amalgamated, suffered the effects of cheap foreign imports and now some don't even produce, letting their farms out to farming contractors. Quarrying too, is much too is less busy meaning more redundant jobs. Like many other parts of the Borders, coal mining was attempted near Whitsome but sadly, the seam was not financially viable. Of course, all that leads to depopulation as people headed for the towns in search of housing and jobs. That in turn leads to the closing of facilities and,

~ *Whitsome* ~

in Whitsome's case, the loss of the old school was a disaster - education which had carried on in the parish for 400 years, for a time in two schools, had come to an end. Later, as we shall see, the kirk too, closed its doors for the last time.

Left:
Whitsome
old mort/watch house
in the
original
graveyard

An early church stood in the vicinity of the old cemetery

Below:
Old headstone of the
White family

Whitsome is indeed an ancient parish and a church existed since before the reign of David I (1124-1153) who's elder brother, Edgar granted the church to Coldingham Priory, by charter, in the first decade of the 12th century, a grant which was reiterated by David and, in later times, confirmed by William I and again by Robert III of Scots in 1392. That early church, it seems, was the direct ancestor of the present church which was built in 1803.

In 1296, the parson of Whitsome, Rauf de Hawden, swore fealty to Edward at Berwick and had his chapel, which had previously been seized by English, restored to his rightful care. Another mentioned by charter in early times was Thomas of Whitsome who witnessed a grant of lands in Roxburghshire.

While Whitsome appeared to be 'bypassed' by many English armies particularly Edward III's church destruction tour of the 14th century and the Rough Wooing Wars of the 16th century, it did suffer damage at the hands of the Duke of Gloucester, later Richard III, when, in 1482, he left barely a house standing during his savage attack of Berwickshire.

The old church, of earthen floor and thatched roof was said to be in a dreadful condition for many years before it was finally replaced. It stood in the old kirkyard, around 200 yards south of the present building though there is no remaining vestige of the old building but many symbolic and other

~ *Whitsome* ~

interesting stones remain in the company of an old watch house which was generally used by bereaved families for a week after the burial of their loved ones in case of attempts to snatch the bodies for medical science which was rife throughout Scotland including Berwickshire.

One of the highlights of the old church arrived in the early 18th century when the indomitable Reverend Thomas Boston was invited to conduct a service there to which hundreds attended, they even caused the roof to collapse as many climbed the walls to catch a glimpse of the original 'fire and brimstone' minister.

The 1803 church with additions in 1912, is essentially a Gothic-style rectangle with a gabled aisle to the north, a square, 3-stage tower topped by the belfry on the south wall and an entry porch in to a vestibule on the west gable. A chancel with adjoining vestry was added to the east wall.

Whitsome Kirk from the roadside

Sadly however, the church has closed, been cleared of all its fittings and is being prepared to be converted to a private residence. It is not an ideal situation but at least the iconic building is being saved for future generations to view and admire. At one point, the parish contained a Secessionist Meeting House at Old Newton which, more than once, hosted the weel kent minister, Henry Erskine, himself a 'trail blazing' clergyman who's sons followed in their father's shoes.

Today's village is a lovely, serene place with a fine variety of houses of all architectural genres; it is a good place to live and raise a family even though the people must travel for most of life's needs, including shopping, banking and work, with children attending Swinton for primary and Berwickshire High School at Duns for their higher education. However the the peace of the village more than compensates for the inevitable daily journeys.

~ *Whitsome – Hilton* ~

Right : As it was

The Nave and the Chancel of Whitsome Parish Church

*H*owever, despite all that has been lost over the years in terms of facilities, the people of Whitsome, have one (or should I say won) a major 'consolation' prize, the Whitsome Ark, the most beautiful and versatile community building in the Scottish Borders. Café, function hall allowing space for most occasions and functions, something for every one in the community. Add all that to the Community Shop with a Post Office and it does not take an expert to appreciate how much closer, and stronger a community becomes when there is a place such as the Ark, where people can meet on a daily basis and discuss whatever comes to mind. This 'back to the future' project deserves every praise and may be a pointer for other communities to follow in the years ahead.

~ *Hilton~*

*B*arely a mile east of Whitsome, lie the scant ruins of the ancient church of Hilton. Like Whitsome, Hilton Church was founded during the 12th century and was consecrated by David de Bernham of St. Andrews in 1243. When the churches united in 1735, the death knell tolled for Hilton Kirk which was allowed to fall in to permanent decay. The kirkyard was used for many years after the closing of the church but sadly is now but a wilderness and the scant remains of the kirk and graveyard, look increasingly lost amf forlorn. By that time, the village was all but gone having suffered the same fate as its 'big brother' along the road in 1482.

*T*he loss of its old school was a savage blow and was probably the final nail in the village's coffin. All that remains of the little town on the hill is a fine

~ Hilton ~

bungalow, two terraces of lovely cottages facing over to the sad sight of the old kirkyard, farm buildings and a fine farmhouse. While all but gone, Hilton's history survives as do some names from early times, indicating the importance of the secluded community. There was Adam de Bernack and Hugh of Hilton who both swore fealty to Edward I in 1296 as did David, John and Robert, all designated of Hilton. Alan was the church priest in 1165 while William de Hilton witnessed charters in 1272 and 1275. Those names and their actions do indicate a place of some importance in medieval Scotland. Sadly that ecclesiastical and political importance has long since passed in to the annals of Berwickshire history but the little hamlet does provide an 'away from it all' residence for the few who are still proud to call Hilton, home.

Right: The Hamlet of Hilton

* * *

Below: last remnants of Hilton Kirk

courtesy of Walter Baxter

Whitsome and Hilton really are lovely, tranquil places, a quiet environ containing a rich variety of atmospheric houses, cottages and a lovely hall, all surrounded by rich farming lands. All is well in this lovely corner of Berwickshire, notwithstanding the loss of their cherished facilities particularly the schools and churches.

~ An after thought ~

We have talked all through the book about old kirks, when they were founded and was there a village nearby? Every one I have mentioned as "being one of the oldest" has a claim to the title of being the very earliest church in the region, only problem is, the evidence, to date, has not been forthcoming but there are precedents in south-east Scotland.

For centuries, it was 'thought' there was an ancient church founded by St. Cuthbert at the ancient village at Whittinghame in the northern Lammermuirs. That was also the case of another truly ancient kirk at Auldhame, on the coast, just south of North Berwick but again, no evidence, at least that was the case until much more recent times.

In both parishes, bones were turned up in the fields and, when the archaeologists moved in, and carried out digs, digs which uncovered some startling facts. In both cases the digs produced Christian burial sites with the bodies laid out east to west and remnants of wooden buildings. At St. Baldred's Auldhame in particular, apart from over 240 burials, laid in a Christian fashion, the stone foundations of a church, similar to the old church at the Hirsel were found. Below the stone foundations, the remains of a wooden church were also found. For so long, people were convinced of the villages and kirks but scant evidence enshrouded their beliefs until the those all important digs. Evidence of wooden cot houses were also uncovered.

It could well be the case that the ancient churches we have visited, are built directly atop the original kirks, keeping their secrets safe, for the time being at least. In the case of Bonkyl for instance, where all evidence of a village has been masked by the sands of time, it may well take a plough to uncover the remains of structures to show us exactly where the old village was. We live on in bewilderment but one day, I am sure, the answer will surely be uncovered. It is almost a case of common sense, no one, but no one, would build a church in the middle of no where, there must have been a community in the immediate vicinity of the old Divine.

On a final note, I would like to offer my grateful thanks to everyone who took the time to talk and who helped make this book possible. I do not have all their names but what I do know is, the people of Berwickshire, once more, have not been found wanting when it comes to helping a total stranger in need, like me.

Thank you all so very much,

James

* * * * *

Bibliography

Title, Author, Date, Publisher
All where appropriate

*History of the Berwickshire's Towns and Villages in the present day – Elizabeth M.W. Layhe 1994 ISBN 978-0952322108 – Entire Productions 1994
*The Churches and Churchyards of Berwickshire – James Robson – J & JH Rutherford, Kelso - 1896
*Portrait of the Border Country – Nigel Tranter – 978-079131403 – Robert Hale, second edition – 1972
*Fasti Ecclessia Scoticannae, Synods of Merse & Teviotdale and Dumfries & Galloway – Volume 11 – Hew Scott DD – Oliver & Boyd, Edinburgh – new edition 1917
*Churches and Graveyards of Berwickshire – G.A.C. Binnie 978-0952680505 – G.A.C. Binnie – 1995
*Berwickshire News bulletins - several
*Lords of Longformacus – www.fionasinclair.co.uk – Fiona Sinclair
*The Cockburn Family – Sir Robert & Harry A. Cockburn – 1913 – T.N. Foulis (Publishers) – London & Edinburgh and printed by T & A Constable, Edinburgh.
*Complete Baronetage 1665-1707 – George E. Cockayne 1904 – Published by William Pollard & Co. Exeter.
*The East Nisbet Conventicle – Reverend John Blackadder – Taken from The Men of the Covenant Volume One – Alexander Smellie – 1908 – Published by Melrose of London
*Rutherford's Southern Counties Register – 1866 – J & J.H. Rutherford – Kelso
*The Record of the Cockburn Family – Sir Robert Cockburn & Harry A. Cockburn – 1913 – T.N. Foulis, London & Edinburgh.
*The Castellated and Domestic Architecture of Scotland from the Twelfth to the Eighteenth Centuries – David Macgibbon & Thomas Ross – 1892 - David Douglas, Edibnurgh
*Village Kirks of the Borders of Scotland 978-1-4477-4393-3 - James Denham – 2011 – Galashiels
*The Scottish Borders, Land of the Horse 978-1-4716-6614-8   James Denham – 2012 - Galashiels
*scottishbordersheritage.co.uk – various
*Marchmont and the Humes of Polwarth - 1894 - Julian Margaret Warrender - Wm. Blackwood & Sons - Edimburgh & London
*The Catholic Encyclopaedia – newadvent.org/ca
*British History Online - Henry VIII - April 1524 pages 24-25
*Ragman's Roll site - rampantscotland.com/ragman/blragman_v.htm

Bibliography (cont)

*The Peerage - thepeerage.com – various
*The family of Corbett: its life and times Volume 2 - ebook ebooksread.com
*Polwarth Parish Church feasability study – robinkent.c
*Langton Church literature
*Langton and Gavinton History – berwickshire-lillies.co.uk/Langton_Gavinton_History.html
*History of Whitsome by Lesley Robertson on Genuki website - genuki.org.uk/big/sct/BEW/Whitsome/history.html
*Caledonia, or an Account, Historical and Topographical of North Britain, from ancient times to the present - George Chalmers - London 1807
*Swinton Church Literature
*Simprim Graveyard Notice
*Fogo Church Literature
*An old Berwickshire town: The history of the town and parish of Greenlaw from the earliest times - Robert Gibson, edited after his death in 1903, by his son, Thomas Gibson – 1905
*Edrom Kirk History : kirkweddings.com/edrom_kirk,history.htm
*History of Edrom – visionofbritain.org.uk
*Ancient Church Dedications in Scotland - James Murray MacKinlay – 1916
*British Listed Buildings Online – various
*Chirnside Parish Church Website - freewebs.com/chirnside_parish_church
*Chirnside Football Club Website – chirnsidefc.co.uk/
*Churches consecrated in Scotland in the 13th century, dates by Rev. William Lockhart - The Proceedings of the Society
*Dunbar Collegiate Church – rosslyntemplars.org.uk
*Kirk of Lammermuir – lammermuirlife.co.uk
*Origines Parochiales Scotiae, the Antiquities Ecclesiastical and Territorial of the Parishes of Scotland, Volume First - Lord Jeffrey - Sir Thomas MakDougall Bart. - The Hon. Charles Francis Stuart - Bannatyne Club - Edinburgh -1851
*History of Bonkle - www.bonkle.org.uk - Sandy McIntyre, compiled by Ian Glen
*The Statistical Accounts of Scotland 1834-1845 - various - Patron, Sir John Archibald Sinclair, 3rd Viscount Thurso
*The Statistical Accounts of Scotland 1792-1799 - various - under the supervision of Sir John Sinclair of Ulbster
*Pigot & Co's New Commercial Directory of Scotland. Edinburgh-Glasgow (and every town, villages and seaport in Scotland) 1825-26

Bibliography (cont)

*People of Medieval Scotland, 1093 -1314 – www.poms.ac.uk (accessed on numerous occasions between March 2015 and January 2016)
*Old maps of Scottish counties – www.maps.nls.uk/counties/index.html
*Ordnance gazetteer of Scotland - Various places - Francis H. Groome 1882
*borderreivers.co.uk/
*Royal Commission on the ancient and historical monuments of Scotland - Canmore and Scotland's Places - various
(scotlandsplaces.gov.uk)
*In the Footsteps of Flodden, 2013 – gathering from Nunraw to Ellemford
*BBC Television, House Detectives – Ellem Lodge
*National Library of Scotland – Town Plans/Views – Duns – John Wood, 1824
*Wikipedia articles where reliable links are available
*Chirnside – www.botany/bay.plus.com/chirnside/welcome
*Marchmont and the Hume of Polwarth – Margaret Warrender - 1894